Scholarly Collaboration
on the Academic Social Web

Synthesis Lectures on Information Concepts, Retrieval, and Services

Editor
Gary Marchionini, *University of North Carolina, Chapel Hill*

Synthesis Lectures on Information Concepts, Retrieval, and Services publishes short books on topics pertaining to information science and applications of technology to information discovery, production, distribution, and management. Potential topics include: data models, indexing theory and algorithms, classification, information architecture, information economics, privacy and identity, scholarly communication, bibliometrics and webometrics, personal information management, human information behavior, digital libraries, archives and preservation, cultural informatics, information retrieval evaluation, data fusion, relevance feedback, recommendation systems, question answering, natural language processing for retrieval, text summarization, multimedia retrieval, multilingual retrieval, and exploratory search.

Scholarly Collaboration on the Academic Social Web

Daqing He and Wei Jeng

ISBN: 978-3-031-01171-9   paperback
ISBN: 978-3-031-02299-9   ebook

DOI 10.1007/978-3-031-02299-9

A Publication in the Springer series
SYNTHESIS LECTURES ON INFORMATION CONCEPTS, RETRIEVAL, AND SERVICES

Lecture #47
Series Editor: Gary Marchionini, *University of North Carolina, Chapel Hill*
Series ISSN
Print 1947-945X   Electronic 1947-9468

Scholarly Collaboration on the Academic Social Web

Daqing He and Wei Jeng
School of Information Sciences, University of Pittsburgh

*SYNTHESIS LECTURES ON INFORMATION CONCEPTS, RETRIEVAL,
AND SERVICES #47*

ABSTRACT

Collaboration among scholars has always been recognized as a fundamental feature of scientific discovery. The ever-increasing diversity among disciplines and complexity of research problems makes it even more compelling to collaborate in order to keep up with the fast pace of innovation and advance knowledge. Along with the rapidly developing Internet communication technologies and the increasing popularity of the social web, we have observed many important developments of scholarly collaboration on the academic social web.

In this book, we review the rapid transformation of scholarly collaboration on various academic social web platforms and examine how these platforms have facilitated academics throughout their research lifecycle—from forming ideas, collecting data, and authoring articles to disseminating findings. We refer to the term "academic social web platforms" in this book as a category of Web 2.0 tools or online platforms (such as CiteULike, Mendeley, Academia.edu, and ResearchGate) that enable and facilitate scholarly information exchange and participation. We will also examine scholarly collaboration behaviors including sharing academic resources, exchanging opinions, following each other's research, keeping up with current research trends, and, most importantly, building up their professional networks.

Inspired by the model developed by Olson et al. [2000] on factors for successful scientific collaboration, our examination of the status of scholarly collaboration on the academic social web has four emphases: technology readiness, coupling work, building common ground, and collaboration readiness. Finally, we talk about the insights and challenges of all these online scholarly collaboration activities imposed on the research communities who are engaging in supporting online scholarly collaboration.

This book aims to help researchers and practitioners understand the development of scholarly collaboration on the academic social web, and to build up an active community of scholars who are interested in this topic.

KEYWORDS

scholarly collaboration, digital scholarship, digital scholar, academic social network, research networks, scholar identity

Contents

Acknowledgments

We would like to thank Professors Brad Hemminger and Mike Thelwall for their invaluable comments and suggestions on this book. This work is partially supported by National Natural Science Foundation of China project "Research on Knowledge Organization and Service Innovation in the Big Data Environments" (#71173249).

Daqing He and Wei Jeng
January 2016

CHAPTER 1

Scholarship in Networked Participatory Environment

1.1 SCHOLARSHIP AND DIGITAL SCHOLARSHIP

1.1.1 SCHOLARSHIP, SCHOLAR ACTIVITIES, AND ICT INFLUENCE ON SCHOLARSHIP

Ernest Boyer [1990] in his "Scholarship Reconsidered" stated that the work of a scholar is "stepping back from one's investigation, looking for connections, building bridges between theory and practice, and communicating ones knowledge effectively to students" (p. 16). This relatively general view of scholarship covers a variety of scholar's interior activities, which include learning an academic topic, reasoning about intellectual problems, and interpreting evidence and results [Borgman, 2015].

In the literature, scholarship is often conflated with the concept of original research. Indeed, while scholarship is a preferred term in humanities, science and social science often use "scholarship" and "research" interchangeably [Borgman, 2015]. However, our view of scholarship is more aligned with Boyer's broader view, although we do acknowledge that original research is a significant part of scholarship. In order to engage scholars in a wide range of disciplines, we use "scholarship" throughout this book.

Furthermore, as a complex and progressive activity, scholarship is increasingly less likely to be "disembodied" and "autonomous," and more like "community-conscious" [Veletsianos and Kimmons, 2012]. This indicates that scholars have to interact with others, such as other scholars, professionals in different sectors, students, and even the general public. Therefore, scholarship could comprise academic activities such as education, scholarly communication, collaboration, and knowledge sharing. This broad view of scholarship is consistent with Boyer's definition of scholarship, and motivated us to examine the essence of scholar activities.

The Essence of Scholar Activities. Many scholars believe that scholarship has some common essential activities across disciplines. Boyer [1990] pointed out four dimensions of scholarship—discovery, integration, application, and teaching—which became the most well-known framework of defining and legitimizing the range of academic practices. Boyer's framework defines the discovery dimension as scholarly investigation to the unknown and to the gaps in human knowledge, which comes very close to what academic people refer to as "research." The integration dimension then pushes the traditional boundary of disciplines and develops interpretation to the outcome that a scholar discovered. Particularly, through integration, scholars can make "connections across the disciplines," place "the specialties in larger context," illuminate "data in a revealing way," and educate "non-specialists" [Boyer, 1990, p. 18]. He includes the application dimension to emphasize that scholars need to engage themselves in the associated academia communities through providing services and being good citizens. Finally, the teaching dimension involves both educating and enticing future scholars. In conclusion, Boyer's framework characterizes that the trend of scholarship is interdisciplinary, interpretive, and integrative.

Following the same idea, Unsworth [2000] proposed seven "scholarly primitives" that represent the "basic functions common to scholarly activity across disciplines, over time, and independent of theoretical orientation." These primitives include discovering, annotating, comparing, referring, sampling, illustrating, and representing.

Both Boyer and Unsworth's work illustrate that scholarship is a complex notion that involves both horizontal and vertical aspects. For the horizontal aspects, scholarship covers humanities, social science, and science, and is also interdisciplinary. On the other hand, scholarship is a continuing process that involves stages, inputs and outputs, research processes, and data lifecycles. Therefore, as scholarship is becoming increasingly interdisciplinary, interpretative, and integrative, scholars need to build their discovery on previous works, collaborating with others to interpret and integrate results. All of this mean that the supports from information and communication technology are increasingly needed.

ICTs and Scholarship. Information and Communication Technology (ICT), according to UNESCO's World Communication and Information Report [1999], covers a "diverse set of technological tools and resources used to communicate, and to create, disseminate, store, and manage information." Although people often associate ICT with computers and the Internet nowadays, scholarship has been supported by various forms of ICT for thousands of years. The invention of languages, writing systems, paper, and printing technologies all contributed to the teaching, application, integration, and discovery dimensions of scholarship.

Modern scholarship relies heavily on information, which increasingly takes the form of digital representation. Therefore, ICT plays critical roles in supporting modern scholarship. According to the research in cyberinfrastructure (see Figure 1.1), ICT forms the underneath foundation layer, on top of which is a middleware layer that provides the services and core network capabilities that most scholar activities rely on. Then on the top of the infrastructure, there is the information and content layer, which consists of scientific databases and digital libraries that are important data resources for scholars [Borgman, 2007, p. 23].

Because of the rapidly developed ICT, scholarship is experiencing dramatic transformations. Faster and cheaper processors enable powerful data processing capabilities, and better and bigger digital storage capacity enables more and more usages of digital mediums, as well as converting analog records into digital mediums. All of these not only facilitate very large scholar content and datasets, and enable content on different media grow exponentially, but also connect more researchers to various networks to build even more powerful infrastructure.

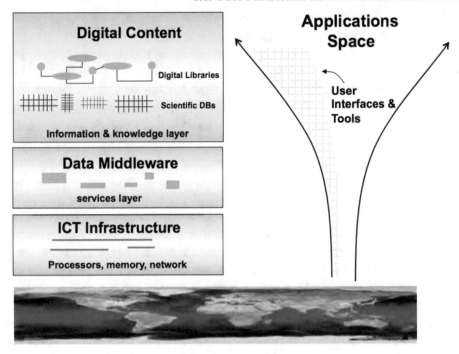

Figure 1.1: Cyberinfrastructure: an evolving view. From Griffin [2013]. Copyright © 2012 Edinburgh University Press. Used with permission.

Within such a new concept, cyberinfrastructure of systems, data, and services, scholars from various disciplines, including science, social science and humanities, all ask the research questions like "(w)hat scholarship becomes possible when, from their desktops, scholars can access vast stores of admittedly highly heterogeneous data together with powerful capabilities for analysis and presentation?" [Friedlander, 2009] Particularly, new research questions often transcend beyond traditional disciplinary boundaries, which then in turn enable research to evolve on a larger scale, becoming richer in languages and communication patterns and more boundaryless in space and time [Friedlander, 2009]. During this process, we witness that scholarship has been influenced by social, economic, technical, and political trends [Borgman, 2007]. Consequently, the nature of scholarship has dramatically changed in the digital age.

1.1.2   DIGITAL SCHOLARSHIP

Digital scholarship combines digital technologies and scholarly activities. Smith Rumsey [2011, p. 2] pointed out some commonly associated technologies include "digital evidence and method, digital authoring, digital publishing, digital curation and preservation, and digital use and reuse of scholarship." This new form of practice affects the whole scholarly process and results in a new model of scholarship called digital scholarship.

Although not all scholars can fully take advantage of the support of digital technologies in their scholarly activities due to various reasons such as locations, disciplines, and economics, digital scholarship increasingly shapes more scholars' research activities or day-to-day decision-making in many ways. For example, Borgman [2007, p. xvii] pointed out that, with digital scholarship, scholars are able to "ask new questions, create new kinds of scholarly products, and reach new audiences." Griffin [2013] commented the basic characteristics of contemporary digital scholarship as "rich dialog, shared and open access to resources and an emphasis on transparency."

Traditionally, the outcome of research often takes the form of formal publications such as monograph, journal articles, and conference papers. Such formal publications still occupy the majority of scholarly products in the current digital scholarship environment. However, increasingly, those products are in digital format and the creation and dissemination of these products are directly supported by ICT. This evolution demonstrates that scholarly activities rely on ICT more and more. As a result, scholars gain more understanding and rely on a successful cyberinfrastructure. For example, more scholars are interested in activities that enable automatic discovery of scholarly products through metadata descriptions, online repositories, and essential computational tool development. Furthermore, there is a feedback loop for these research products because most of them are integrated back to the cyberinfrastructure to improve the overall research capabilities. The formal academic publishing cycle has been greatly shortened as well with article submission, peer-review, manuscript typesetting, and official publishing all happening online at one or two central managed sites [Borgman, 2007]. Recent movements on open access further enable a much wider range of scholars and the public to access and utilize scholarly products.

Digital scholarship also has profound influence on scholarly informal communication. Although scholars can informally communicate with each other before, it is in current ICT supports that scholars can informally exchange information with a great variety of communication tools (e.g., emails, online chat, video conferencing tools, etc.) and online academic social networking sites such as Mendeley, ResearchGate, and Academic.edu.

Digital technology enables a new form of scholarship called open education. First, teaching materials in open education, which mostly rely on the products of scholarship, are either being digitized or born with digital form so that students can easily access them online at any place at any time [Greenhow et al., 2009]. Second, the delivery methods are extended to include either online components or entirely online. More recent MOOC movement further expands the scale of online education utilizing digital technology. All of these engagements of digital scholarship in education provide "more openness and transparency in the public sphere." [Pearce et al., 2012, p. 37].

More interestingly, as various social media applications grow over the Web in recent years, Social Web 2.0 becomes a combination of ICT and web design that aims to enhance participation and collaboration, secure information sharing, and thus further enable creativity on the

Web. Because of this, the whole academic information environment has become more vibrant, social, and participatory too [Andersen, 2007]. Therefore, digital scholarship has another interesting development, that is, to take advantage of social features on the social web to engage in the collaboration aspects of digital scholarship.

1.2   SCHOLARLY COLLABORATION

1.2.1   DEFINITION OF SCHOLARLY COLLABORATION

As Borgman [2007] points out, scholarly collaboration is probably the most studied scholar activity, yet we still have many things unclear about it. On the one hand, scholars compete in priority of discovery, opportunities for funding and awards, venues of publications, and authority in the community. However, on the other hand, the majority scholars are eager to build up academic connections, team up with other scholars to study complex problems, and share scarce data or expensive equipments [Borgman, 2007, p. 169]. In other word, scholarly collaboration is common and increasing. One visible indicator for scholarly collaboration [Cronin et al., 2003] is co-authorship of academic articles. For instance, the number of co-authors per article in bio-medical fields has steadily increased since the 1950s, from 1.9 (pre–1975) to 5.14 (2010–2014).

Furthermore, scholarly collaboration is getting increasingly interdisciplinary. With many years of advancement, most academic problems attracting scholars to work on are complex problems that require deep knowledge on many disciplines. Scholars therefore have the tendency to collaborate with others whose domain expertise could help them solving the problem. For example, through analyzing 1000 academic articles published in 1992 that cover 5 disciplines—chemistry, earth sciences, engineering, mathematics, and medical sciences—Qin et al. [1997] found that the levels and types of interdisciplinary collaboration varied among these disciplines, but the general trend toward high interdisciplinarity was clear. More recently, Bronstein [2003] constructed an interdisciplinary collaboration model that includes five components: interdependence, newly created professional activities, flexibility, collective ownership of goals, and reflection on process. She further identified four factors that influence interdisciplinary collaboration: professional role, structural characteristics, personal characteristics, and history of collaboration. Van Rijnsoever and Hessels [2011] also confirmed several factors that affect interdisciplinary scholarly collaboration: senior scholars being more like to collaborate within discipline and interdisciplinaryly; work experience in firms or governmental organizations increasing the propensity of interdisciplinary collaborations, but decreasing that of disciplinary collaborations; and disciplinary collaborations occurring more frequently in basic disciplines whereas interdisciplinary collaborations happening more in strategic disciplines.

Along with the existing web infrastructure making it easier for scholars to collaborate, scholars also are increasingly willing to share their knowledge and findings. By disseminating published work, preprints, and opinion pieces, scholars are recognizing the benefits of being able to relate to other researchers or communities for exchanging information and knowledge.

1.2.2 SCHOLARLY COLLABORATION ON THE SOCIAL WEB

The social web, as Jenkins et al. [2009] pointed out, includes technologies that shape a participatory culture for everybody, which affect both our everyday life and working environment. This shared culture then helps to develop a form of scholarship called *networked participatory scholarship* [Veletsianos and Kimmons, 2012], which relates to an emergent emphasis on the aggregations of "the actions of individuals that are organized in a complex manner to benefit those individuals." Networked participatory scholarship is a new form of scholarly collaboration on the social web.

To some degree, Boyer's view of scholarship as community-conscious is only profoundly realized in digital scholarship on the social web. Among the scholarly activities mentioned by Boyer, scholarly communication, education, and scholarly collaboration are all related to the communities.

ICT and Scholarly Collaboration. Information and communication technologies have been playing important roles in the rapid development of digital scholarship. The interesting question therefore is whether or not these technologies would facilitate scholarly collaboration as well. The literature indeed provides strong evidence on the influence of ICT to scholarly collaboration. For example, Oxford Internet Institute's report demonstrated that a wide range of collaborative research activities are commonly performed on the Internet [David and Spence, 2003]. Borgman [2007, p. 171] also stated that scholarly collaboration in a distributed environment "rely heavily on information and communication technologies." Furthermore, collaborations with the help of ICT encouraged not only interdisciplinary research but also a broad inventory of partners who would have difficulty conducting research on their own [Borgman, 2007, p. 169]. We also see different models have been proposed for this "electronic communication of scholarly information" [Garvey and Griffith, 1972, Hurd, 2000, Lancaster, 1978]. In summary, the use of ICT, such as email, instant messages, phone conferences, and video-conferences, did automatically give scholars "an added advantage [to collaboration]" [Cummings and Kiesler, 2005, p. 718].

In Chapter 2, we will present a detailed review of technology developed in the academic social web for supporting scholarly collaboration.

1.2.3 FACTORS FOR SUCCESSFUL SCHOLARLY COLLABORATION ON THE SOCIAL WEB

As a type of scholarly activity, scholarly collaboration will generate outcomes that can be measured as success or failure in the academic environment. However, measuring success is not easy. As Olson et al. [2008] pointed out, although success traditionally is measured in terms of productivity, awards, honors, impact factors of the publication venues, or citation counts, scholars and policymakers acknowledge that these measures are "inadequate to assess the full spectrum of goals" of many scholar collaborations, particularly the collaborations on the academic social web, which are new and still rapidly evolving.

Successful Scientific Collaboration. Nevertheless, success should still be the goal of a scholarly collaboration and it is important to examine the factors that can affect the success of a scholarly collaboration. Olson et al. [2000] identified four factors that are critical for collaboration success. Such factors are examined in collaboration with distance technologies, which, although did not include the social web, should still be a relevant starting point for examining the success of scholarly collaboration on the academic social web. These four factors are: common ground, coupling work, collaborative readiness, and technical readiness.

Common Ground. Common ground refers to whether collaborators share common vocabularies and take the same working belief or management style. It is a character sharing among team members, and it covers a range of concepts such as "a common vocabulary" and "prior experience working together" Borgman [2007, p. 171]. According to Clark and Brennan [1991], building common ground can be affected by several important features in the collaboration environment, including:

- co-presence: same physical environment;

- visibility: visible to each other;

- audibility: speech;

- contemporarily: message received immediately;

- simultaneity: both speakers can send and receive;

- sequentially: turns cannot get out of sequence;

- reviewability: able to review other's messages; and

- revisability: can revise messages before they are sent.

At the same time, through affecting these environment features, various communication technologies can contribute differently in building common ground. For example, Olson et al. [2000, p. 160] listed the contributions of some communication technologies in achieving common ground in current environment (see Table 1.1). Certainly, Table 1.1 focuses on common ground in a generic setting, whereas scholarly collaboration on the academic social web may rely on different technologies to build common ground. Furthermore, we acknowledge that communication technologies have evolved greatly in the past 15 years, which changes the characteristics of some communication technologies. For example, some current sophisticated versions of video conferencing could enable some form of co-presence feelings even though it did not provide co-presence experience in the 2000s.

Coupling in Work. The concept of "coupling" characterizes the extent and the kind of communication required by the collaboration work. Therefore, this factor actually examines the nature of the work with the intention to evaluate whether the work is unambiguous, whether the work

Table 1.1: Different technologies in contributions to achieve common ground

Medium	Co-presence	Visibility	Audibility	Co-temporality	Simultaneity	Sequentiality	Reviewability	Re-visibility
Face-to-face	X	X	X	X	X	X		
Telephone			X	X	X	X		
Video Conference		X	X	X	X	X		
Two-way Chat				X	X	X	X	X
Asnwering Machine			X			X		
E-mail							X	X
Letter							X	X

Source: Redraw by Olson et al. [2000, p. 160].

is dividable, and whether the work is tightly coupled that requires constant communication and negotiation [Olson et al., 2000]. Some work can be easily divided into mutually independent components so that not much collaboration or communication is required, whereas some others demand extensive and constant communication. Olson et al. [2000, p. 162] further provided a classification of the work based on their ability for coupling.

- Tightly coupled work: the work that strongly depends on the talents of scholars to achieve collaboration, and is non-routine or even ambiguous.

- Loosely coupled work: the work that has fewer dependencies, or is more routine.

Collaboration Readiness. Collaboration readiness examines the motivation for scholars to collaborate with each other. This comes from either scholars' inner motivations that make them feel ready to collaborate or the discipline norm as well as the work setting that "engender a willingness to share" [Olson and Olson, 2000, p. 164]. The collaboration readiness can also be relevant to whether scholars share a common goal, and trust each other to be reliable to work with.

Technology Readiness. Technology readiness reveals the availability and the reliabilities of technologies that provide appropriate support for scholars to collaborate in their working environment. The technology readiness can be further divided into the appropriate functionalities, ease of use, and comfort of the relevant technologies.

In the field of information science and behavioral science, we have seen researchers adopt these four factors when discussing the essence of scholarly collaboration and communication [Borgman,

2007]. Later, in 2008, Olson and his research team came up with Theory of Remote Scientific Collaboration (TORSC), which extends the research context in their previous framework [Olson et al., 2000] to general collaborations. The updated framework is comprised of five overarching categories: the nature of work, common ground, collaboration readiness, technology readiness, and management/planning/decision making [Olson et al., 2008, p. 80].

Our discussion in this book consults both of Olson's models. However, we decided to exclude the management/planning/decision-making factor in this book because scholarly collaboration on the academic social web is still relatively simple and ad hoc, which makes the management factor relatively less developed comparing to the other four factors.

Embedded Knowledge. Besides Olson & Olson's [2000] model, Kanfer & Haythornthwaite [2000] proposed the factors affecting distance collaboration from the view point of knowledge processing. They pointed out three important factors for collaboration: knowledge characteristics, group context, and communication infrastructure. In their model, knowledge characteristics include "paradigmatic consensus," one domain or multidisciplinary area, the research outcomes and research design (e.g., "[if] is recoverable through ethnographic analysis"). The group context includes the social structure of the team, the interactive process of the team that collaborators interact throughout the research process, and prior outcomes or experience [Kanfer et al., 2000, p. 320]. The communication infrastructure considers the technologies and channels that support knowledge process "such as documents, electronic mail, teleconferences, videoconferences (p. 320)."

Based on both Olson & Olson's model as well as Kanfer & Haythornthwaite's model, we propose a factor schema. As shown in Table 1.2, our factor schema tries to draw inputs from both models, and have direct mapping to Olson et al. [2000]'s model, but it is also in consideration of scholarly collaboration activities on the academic social web. In the remaining chapters, we will cover each of these factors with one chapter, respectively.

1.3 SUMMARY

This chapter started with the introduction of scholarship, digital scholarship, and scholar collaboration, and ended with the presentation of a schema for examining the factors affecting scholarly collaboration on the academic social web. In the remainder of this book, we will utilize the schema to organize the presentation of scholars' collaboration behaviors and examine the support of platforms on the academic social web.

During the discussion in the remainder of this book, we will examine scholars' collaboration with one another as well as with the general public in research projects. As stated in this chapter, scholars' collaborative behaviors can be enabled or constrained by technology readiness in those academic social platforms. Therefore, our discussion of the four factors influencing scholarly col-

Table 1.2: An overview of book chapters

Our Categories (He and Jeng)	Olson and Olson	Kanfer and Haythornthwaite
Collaboration readiness for Social Scholarly Collaboration	Collaboration readiness	—
Chapter 3: Coupling work for Social Scholarly Collaboration	Coupling (dependencies) in Work	Knowledge characteristics
Chapter 4: Common ground for Social Scholarly Collaboration	Common Ground	Group Context
Chapter 2: Technical readiness for Social Scholarly Collaboration	Collaboration technology readiness	Communication infrastructure (technology, as Borgman cited in Borgman, 2007)

laboration will start with presenting technology readiness, then examine the nature of academic works that scholars conducted on the social web (i.e., coupling in work), and finally move to the two factors related to scholars themselves—building common ground and their collaboration readiness.

CHAPTER 2

Technology Readiness for Social Scholarly Collaboration

Besides using generic social media platforms such as Twitter and Facebook for their scholarly collaborations, scholars are observed to use online services that are specifically designed for them and their academic activities. These services have been identified in different domains, which include Academic Social Networking by researchers in informational science [Jeng et al., 2015, Thelwall et al., 2013], Networked Participatory Scholarship by education researchers [Veletsianos and Kimmons, 2012], and Research Networking (RN) tools in health science related fields [Schleyer et al., 2008, Weber et al., 2011].

Citation-based bibliometric methods have been widely used to evaluate scholars for hiring, tenure, promoting, or other rewards and recognition [Borgman, 2007]. Before the emergence of academic social media platforms, scholars relied on tools such as Web of Science (WoS) to access information of citation counts and scholar impacts. The interaction between scholars, if any, was indirect.

A decade ago, with the rise of web technologies such as Google Scholar or Microsoft Academic Search, scholars were getting more options to keep a close watch at others' latest research progress. At the same time, web-based citation tools such CiteULike, BibSonomy, and RefWorks were also growing in population. Although these platforms can provide features such as social bookmarking, publication sharing, and citation management, they usually lack scholar identity and collaboration functions.

In this chapter, we review technology functionalities for supporting scholarly collaboration in academic social web platforms. In the reviewing of the technology readiness, we pay specific attention to key technology functions that could affect scholarly collaboration. In order to reveal more structure in these key technology features, we group them into the following three functional blocks:

- functional block for establishing scholars' online profiles;

- functional block for collaborating with peer scholars; and

- mechanisms for engaging general public.

As shown in Table 2.1, social platforms supporting scholarly collaboration could exhibit some or all of the three functional blocks.

Table 2.1: Categories of technology functional blocks for scholarly collaboration on academic social web platforms

Functional Blocks/Mechanisms	Functions	Characteristics
Establishing scholars' online identity	Supporting research tasks	Support day-to-day research tasks
	Developing profile and reputation	Shared individual context and building mutual understanding
	Registering scholarly work	• Pre-register scholarly work in public sphere • Fast, alternative channel for disseminating research materials and products
Collaborating with peer scholars	Developing relationship with peer researchers	• Mechanism that allows for socializing • Building mutual understanding
	Grouping and co-production	• Gather academics or discipline group • Allowing discussions
	Information exchange	Instant peer feedback
	Building conversations	• Synchronous video and audio transmissions • Known identity asynchronous conversion
Engaging general public	Crowd-sourcing	Crowdsourcing and crowdfunding
	Citizen science platforms	Platforms that deepen citizen-academia relationship

2.1   FUNCTIONAL BLOCK FOR ESTABLISHING SCHOLARS' ONLINE IDENTITY

Many scholars use social media not only for personal networking but also for promoting their own research. CIBER at University College London (as cited in Rowlands et al., 2011) conducted a survey of scholars in worldwide, and found that nearly 80% of scholars from 14 disciplines have used social media tools in their research process. Not surprisingly, in the survey the most helpful function for scholars to use social media is disseminating research findings. This finding is also identified by Jeng et al. [2015], which suggests that most users on academic social media focused on the research features, such as dissemination, annotation, document management, and article recommendation, rather than forming a group or developing their professional network.

While research promotion is usually considered as a social media usage that benefits scholars individually (rather than seeking potential collaborators or forming a community), it is in fact an indispensable step toward scholarly collaboration. By registering and prompting their own research work, scholars establish their public research profile as well as their reputation in the virtual online environment, which then enables the mutual discovery potential collaborators via a few keystrokes.

2.1.1   THE FUNCTION FOR SUPPORTING RESEARCH TASKS

The first function in establishing scholars' online identity is to support scholars' individual tasks. In the context of the academic social web, supporting research tasks can be instantiated into features like article discovery, document management, and citation management. These features overall present the scholars' research outcomes in terms of publications and the scholars' research interests in terms of the articles that they cite.

Table 2.2: Summary of key features of the function for supporting research tasks

Function	Key Features	General Descriptions	Feature Examples
Supporting research tasks	Article discovery	This feature allows users to search for relevant articles using keywords. The site can also actively recommend new articles to users.	Mendeley Paper Search, Academia.edu, ResearchGate, F1000, Research4life.org
	Document management (PDF)	This feature allows users to establish a personal library that organizes articles in a structural manner.	Mendeley Web Library, Mendeley Desktop, Zotero Desktop
	Citation management	This feature helps users manage the bibliographic database, providing a convenient tool by which users can insert or modify the citations in writing.	Mendeley, Zotero

Article Discovery. Article discovery is a basic function in academic social networks because it is an important scholar task. It can be implemented either reactively or proactively. A keyword-based search is an example of reactive article discovery where users directly retrieve relevant articles at local or online libraries. In contrast, article recommendation is an example of proactive article discovery where potential interesting articles are suggested to the scholars based on their identified interests.

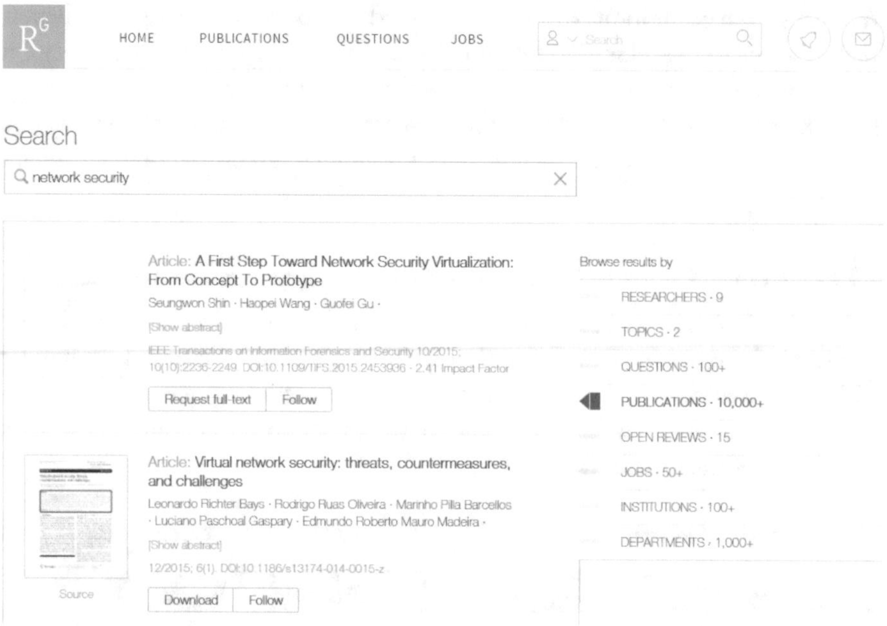

Figure 2.1: RG allows users to browse results by different types of resource.

There is no standard implantation of article discovery. Different academic social websites could provide different interpretation of article discovery. For example, Mendeley and Research-Gate, two very popular academic social networking sites, both provide a keyword-based search. Depending on inputting queries, such a feature provides scholars the opportunities for either exploring articles in broad topic or articles satisfying specific needs. The article search in ResearchGate (RG) stays at simplest a basic keyword search, but Mendeley puts more emphasis on scholars' querying capabilities so that it provides an advanced search option. Even though RG only offers basic search, it has "one-stop" searching feature, where a browse pane is displayed with the article search results to allow scholars to select certain facets such as relevant open reviews or questions in Research Q&A. Figure 2.1 illustrates different search results in various categories, such as publications, questions, open reviews, job openings, etc., while using the keywords "network security."

However, it should be clearly recognized that article discovery in academic social websites such as Mendeley and ResearchGate is different than those in generic search engines such as Google. This is because academic social sites rely on scholars' generated content so that only the articles that have been added to the academic social site can be retrieved and displayed as the results of article discovery. Therefore, article discovery in academic social sites should not be viewed as a comprehensive search of the whole literature body [Bar-Ilan, 2012].

Document Management. The question of how to manage the large quantity of collected and published articles is a very common problem for scholars. Different to the popularity of the article discovery feature, document management only exists in a few academic social networking services, such as Zotero and Mendeley. A metadata exacter in document management plays an important role so that the descriptions of the documents can be constructed automatically. For example, while a document management tool receives a PDF file from a scholar's drag and drop action, it extracts important bibliographic information such as title, authors, publication year, venue, volume, and issue number. In addition, document management feature in several academics social networking services support document synchronization between the PDF libraries on multiple devices, and many of them also support scholars' annotation of documents, such as highlighting text and inserting notes.

Citation Management. Likewise, some academic social tools allow users to manage their citations. Citation management is not a new feature. Before the social web, Endnote and Refwork were often used by scholars as their local reference tools. However, more recent versions of citation management features are implemented on the academic social web with strong social characteristics. Their examples include social reference tools such as CiteUlike and BibSonomy to community-based reference tools such as Mendeley and Zotero. Often, citation management and document management are integrated together in one site. These citation management tools support metadata extraction from the import from various sources such as Bibtex or PDF's metadata. Such tools can also be implemented as flexible plug-ins to be embedded into web browsers or word editing tools. As web-based services, the interoperation is considered too, so that citation information can be easily converted from the format of one site such as Endnotes to the format of another site such as Mendeley. However, as the function based on social user-generated content, the information collected in citation management tools is far from error-free, and could potentially have many duplicates.

2.1.2 DEVELOPING PROFILE AND REPUTATION

Creating profiles is usually the first step of using a generic social networking service, which is also a very common feature for most academic social networking sites [Boyd and Ellison, 2008]. After creating a profile, social networking sites usually allow users to monitor their personal metrics (e.g., Facebook's Insights) by providing information about a profile's statistics and traffic. In this section, we walk through several such features like the profile, reputation mechanism, report of impact, and endorsement system to highlight the importance of identity management in the academic social web (see Table 2.3).

The need of scholar identification has been widely recognized for a long time. In addition to social media profiles described above, several organizations are also promoting dedicated scholar identity systems. Thomson Reuters has long been known for promoting the ResearcherID system, which is now integrated with ORCID and Web of Science (WoS) system. ORCID, as a unique identifier, aims at solving the identification problem of academic authors. This approach also aims

Table 2.3: Summary of key features of the technologies for developing identity and reputation

Function	Key Features	General Descriptions	Feature Examples
Developing Profile and Reputation	Profiles	Feature that allows users to build their prole with academic properties.	Academia.edu, RG, Mendeley
	Impact report	Feature that gathers usage reports for users.	Academia.edu, Altmetric, ImpactStory, ResearchGate, ResearcherID, Google Scholar
	Incentive reputation mechanism	A mechanism that encourages users to engage the service. Usually contribution level-up system. Sometimes a website allows users to recommend other users for their skills and expertise.	RG Score, LinkedIn, Mendeley, Impactstory

for managing academic "records of research activities (including publications, datasets, patents etc.)" [Haustein and Larivière, 2015, p. 127].

Profile with Academic Properties. The profile is probably the only mechanism for a scholar to establish his/her identity and reputation in an online community, and it is the most important resource for other researchers to check whether or not to collaborate with this scholar. In the academic social web, the available academic properties for scholars to develop their profiles include a lot of different information, and often different academic social networking sites have different emphasis (see Table 2.4).

Social sites usually have built-in incentive mechanisms to encourage users' engagement and content contribution. Particularly, these incentive mechanisms are designed to encourage content creation and user interaction. However, at the same time, such incentive mechanisms can be converted into reputation system for scholars in the sites.

Impact Reports. After creating a profile, a scholar could receive a personal impact report from the academic social site. We observed two types of impact reports. The first one is an on-site report. For example, ResearchGate and Academia.edu provide some common metrics used in their impact reports: Publication downloads, Publication views, Citations, Profile views, Followers, or Readership.

The second type gathers several sites' metrics to build up scholars' impact reports. For example, Altmetric (altmetric.com) is an online tool that tracks activities around a scholarly content,

Table 2.4: Research-oriented properties in academic social networking platforms Note: Required properties are shown in navy; available properties in light green (as of November 2015)

Medium	Real Name	Bio	Current Affiliation	Honors and Awards	Disclipine	Advisor	Publications	Research Interest (shown as keywords)	Pre-print Full-text	CV (file)	Education Backgrounds	Skills	Co-authors	Research Experience	Membership (professional society)
Face-to-face	■	⊙	⊙			⊙	⊙	⊙	⊙	⊙			⊙		
Telephone	■	⊙	⊙	⊙	■	⊙	⊙	⊙	⊙		⊙	⊙	⊙	⊙	⊙
Video Conference	■	⊙	⊙		■	⊙	⊙							⊙	
Two-way Chat	■	⊙			⊙	⊙	⊙						⊙		
Answering Machine	■	⊙	⊙	⊙		⊙	⊙				⊙	⊙	⊙	⊙	⊙
E-mail	⊙	⊙	⊙		⊙										

which can be a scholarly product such as a journal article or dataset. As shown in Figure 2.2, the Altmetric detail page lists out statistics of various sources, including relevant mentions from social networking sites (e.g., Twitter, Facebook, and Google+), readership in online reference managers (e.g., Mendeley, CiteULike), blogs, Wikipedia, newspaper, and many other sources. [Altmetric, 2015]. The Altmetric score, which is shown as the number in the circle of the top left corner in Figure 2.2, is generated by the company's algorithm combining various sources into account.

Another example, Impactstory, helps scholars to monitor the verity of impacts of "all their research products—from traditional ones like journal articles, to emerging products such as blog posts, datasets, and software" [Inpactstory, n.d.].

Impact reports are related to an active research topic on the academic social web called *altmetrics*, which refers to "the creation and study of new metrics based on the social web for analyzing scholarship" [Priem et al., 2012]. In addition to using citations for measuring scholarly impact, altmetrics examines certain users' activities on the social web as the indicators of the quality of scholarly products. For example, the counts of users' bookmarks in social reference websites (such as CiteULike) or that of the tags in social networking sites can be used to evaluate

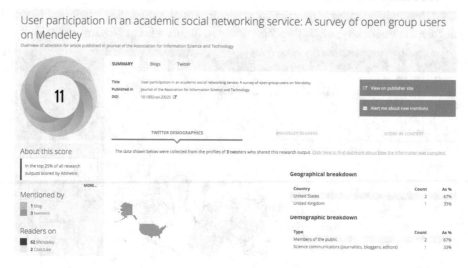

Figure 2.2: An example of Altmetric's details page.

the authors of the articles' research impacts. Instances of data source collected from social media included blogs [Shema et al., 2012], BibSonomy bookmarks [Moilanen et al., 2012], CiteULike bookmarks [Li et al., 2011], Mendeley reader counts [Bar-Ilan et al., 2012, Li et al., 2011], and Twitter mentions [Eysenbach, 2011]. These studies found that some of the altmetrics are highly correlated with the traditional publication indicators, which normally take years to accumulate.

While most of the studies mentioned above collected or analyzed solely single case, Thelwall et al. [2013] compared 11 social media websites with the citations in the Web of Science database, and suggested that not all kinds of social media are suitable for being an indicator to estimate scholarly impacts. In particular, evidence was insufficient for LinkedIn, Pinterest, social Q&A sites, and Reddit because of the lack of research components. Among all other websites with sufficient instances, mentions from Google+ were not significantly correlated with the Web of Science citations. These suggest that using data from some social media can be early indicators of article impact and usefulness, whereas not every source drawn from social media can successfully predict future citations.

Studying altmetrics has become a very active research focus in terms of studying the relationship between social media and scholarly communication. However, user studies on scholars' activities and usage of these altmetrics research sites are nearly absent. Thus, there is little known about how and why academic users utilize the bookmark functions and how these functions can benefit their research experiences. In other words, many researchers use altmetrics data such as CiteULike's bookmarks and Mendeley's reader counts to render research without really knowing who use it and why. Hence, user studies or field studies on these altmetrics websites are very much needed as a background and legitimization for what the intention and who the user group is that scholars are measuring.

Due to the focus of this book, we will not talk further on altmetrics. Readers who are interested in further reading of this topic should consult Priem et al. [2012], Thelwall et al. [2013], and Haustein et al. [2014]. Also, researchers can engage in further technical discussion in professional interest groups such as ASIST's Sig Met (an academic community studying almetrics).

Incentive Mechanisms. Academic social web sites have developed various incentive mechanisms. One typical approach is a scoring system like the RG score in ResearchGate. The RG Score is a score (0–100) calculated based on the number of publications that a user uploads, the questions a user posts, the answers a user responds, and the number of followers a user have [*ResearchGate*, n.d.]. Users could gain their RG scores from two actions: (1) adding more publications into their profiles; and (2) participating the online communities by asking or answering others' questions. However, further study is required to understand to what extent a site can benefit from such a scoring system. While several studies used RG score to measure the scholarly impact for institutional rankings and individuals [Campos and Valencia, 2015, Hoffmann et al., 2015, Thelwall and Kousha, 2015], researchers criticized RG score as "flawed and contradicts the established scientific ranking systems provided by other, much more respected sources" [Tausch, 2014, para 2].

2.1.3   REGISTERING SCHOLARLY WORK

Following the basic mission of scholarly communication [Borgman, 2007], legitimating scholarly outcomes "incorporates authority, quality control and registry in scholarly record" (p. 130). Registering scholarly work in public sphere became a common activity in the current academic social web.

The second common incentive mechanism is to confer honorary titles on early adopter groups. These early users, usually called "advisors" in academic social networking sites, help spread the word regularly maintain their ASNS profiles, or even help organize production demonstrations. In return, these "advisors" will receive some special benefits regarding to the product, such as a free subscription or receiving more available space in ASNS. For example, Mendeley users who help promote the Mendeley site can put on their profile a special badge called "Mendeley advisor." In Impactstory, a member can become an advisor and receive a free subscription.

Developing Research Product List. Scholars often maintain a research product list on academic social websites. These sites provide three types of supports with different levels of automation. In the first type, the sites expose high automation and allow scholars' little control over the profiles. One typical example is *My Citations* in Google Scholar. Scholars can elect to claim their Google Scholar profiles (shown as a publication list). However, once a profile is claimed, Google will automatically build and maintain the profile for the scholar. The only thing that a scholar can do is to edit or remove some metadata of the publication list. The second type of sites gives scholars more controllability, where the scholars can approve or disapprove the addition of documents into their publication list. For example, ResearchGate notifies scholars that "We found a match!" and

Table 2.5: Summary of key features for registering scholarly work

Function	Key Features	General Descriptions	Feature Examples
Registering scholarly work	Developing research product list	Feature that displays academic's publications and related hyperlinks such as the number of readers.	Google Scholar-My Citations, Mendeley, ResearchGate
	Disseminate scholarly work	Feature that helps scholars disseminate published work, preprints.	ResearchGate, Academia.edu, arXiv.org

let the scholar to decide whether or not to add the document. The third type gives scholars all the control to manually add and maintain their profiles. Mendeley falls into this last type.

Disseminate Scholarly Work. Through disseminating their research outcomes, scholars are able to spread their ideas and contribute to the community knowledge in their related disciplines. Traditionally, academic libraries and archives played the primary roles of collecting, accessing, and preserving scholars' research outcomes, particularly print-based officially published materials. However, in the current academic social web, multiple parties from much broader academic spectrum, which include individual scholars, academic intuitions, journal publishers and professional associations, all take some responsibilities for the disseminating scholarly works.

Therefore, academic libraries play much less significant roles in preserving scholarly work, and publishers are not the only gatekeepers in scholarly communication in terms of the process of publishing, disseminating, and archiving research works. There are increasing debates and discussions over the possibilities of new publishing models. Particularly, although social web techniques and sites can facilitate the process of preserving and disseminating scholarly publications, individuals can also publish, deposit, and disseminate their work on the Web. Furthermore, the boundary between scholarly writing, publishing, and disseminating are increasingly vague in the age of social media—when people finish writing and submit their blogs, they publish and distribute it spontaneously.

For example, arXiv.org (pronounced "archive") is an archive for electronic preprints of research articles. When preprints are submitted to arXiv, they will receive an arXiv article id as an object identifier, which enables authors to disseminate their articles before being officially published. Once the article is in arXiv.org, it can start to accumulate early citations. These arXiv links can be distributed and disseminated using social media such as Twitter. This preprint-plus-social-media model allows scholars to easily promote their research work and reach a large number of researchers.

Disseminating scholarly work is also dependent on publishers' self-archiving policy. Depending on the publishers' different policies, scholars may or may not be able to deposit their manuscripts on academic social media sites such as ResearchGate and Academia.edu.

Table 2.6 summarizes the self-archiving policy for journal articles of four major journal publishers, namely, *Elsevier's Policies–Article Sharing* [n.d.], *Springer's Self-archiving Policy* [n.d.], *Wiley's self-archiving policy* [n.d] , and *Sage's Policy of Copyright and Permissions* [n.d.]. These policies regulate documents at different stages, including pre-print (i.e., submitted version, without peer-review), accepted manuscript (peer-reviewed version, without copywriter's editing), and published journal article (the final version). For submitted versions, none of these publishers pose restrictions on article sharing; that is, the publishers either mention explicitly that sharing pre-print documents is allowed (Elsevier and Wiley) or mention no restriction at all (Springer and Sage). Therefore, for the common practices, authors seem to be allowed to register their manuscript at any repository or their personal websites, including academic social media repositories such as ResearchGate and Academia.edu.

For accepted (peer-reviewed) versions, publishers pose more restrictions, but are quite open toward the social media trend. Elsevier explicitly allows sharing articles on certain academic social media sites (e.g., Mendeley, which was acquired by Elsevier in April 2013) with which Elsevier has prior agreement [Elsevier, n.d.]. Springer allows sharing at any repository after a 12-month embargo period, and Wiley also allows sharing at non-profit repositories after the embargo period. However, it is still unclear whether academic social media such as ResearchGate and Academia.edu are considered non-profit repositories (or whether or not they are considered as a repository). Finally, for published versions, none of these publishers allow uploading full-text. Therefore, it can be problematic to upload the final published articles to academic social websites.

2.2   FUNCTIONAL BLOCK FOR COLLABORATING WITH PEER SCHOLARS

Scholars need help from the academic social web not only in constructing their online identity for preparing online scholarly collaboration (as described in Section 2.1), but also in facilitating the collaboration directly. This is because online scholarly collaboration is a new form of academic activity, and both scholars and the academic social websites are in the process of exploring the optimal mechanisms. We categorize the direct supports from academic social websites to scholarly collaboration into three types: developing relationship among scholars (Section 2.2.1), forming interest groups for co-production (Section 2.2.2), and exchanging information among scholars (Section 2.2.3).

2.2.1   DEVELOPING RELATIONSHIP

Our review of generic social media services shows that users can form relationships through being friends (contacts), following or being followed (follower), and endorsement. This is true on the academic social web for scholars' relationships too. Contacts is a mutual relationship that is common at the early stage of the academic social web. For example, both LinkedIn and early Mendeley (prior to March 2014) have "Contacts," which require mutual agreements via invi-

Table 2.6: Major journal publishers' self-archiving policy for subscribed journal *(Continues.)*

	Pre-prints (submitted version)	Accepted Manuscripts (peer-reviewed version)	Published Journal Articles
Elsevier	Authors can share their preprints any-where at any time.	Authors can immediately share this version: • On authors' non-commercial personal homepage or blog • By updating a preprint in arXiv or RePEc • On their institutional repository for internal institutional uses or as part of an invitation-only research collaboration group • Sharing to their students, colleagues, or to research collaborators for their personal use • By private scholarly sharing as part of an invitation-only work group on commercial sites with which Elsevier has an agreement (i.e., Mendeley) After the embargo period (varies, usu-ally 12-24 months, 36-48 months for some specic journals): • Non-commercial hosting platforms such as their institutional repository (doesn't have to be internal use anymore). • Commercial sites with which Elsevier has an agreement	Share link instead of the full-text
Springer	Does not mention any restriction	Authors can immediately share this version: • On their own websites • After the embargo period (12 months): • At any repository	

Table 2.6: *(Continued.)* Major journal publishers' self-archiving policy for subscribed journal

	Pre-prints (submitted version)	Accepted Manuscripts (peer-reviewed version)	Published Journal Articles
Wiley	Authors can share their preprint at: • the author's personal website • the author's company/institution • not-for-prifit subject-based preprint servers or repositories	After the embargo period (varies, 12-24 months), the author can share the accepted version at: • the author's personal website • the author's company/institutional repository or archive • not-for-prot subject-based repositories	N/A
Sage	Does not mention any restriction	On author's own personal websites, department's website, or the repository of the author's institution without any restrictions.	N/A

tations. However, nowadays the follower system, which is a directional relationship, is getting its popularity. The example academic social websites that have implemented the follower system include ResearchGate, Google Scholar Citations, Academia.edu, Zotero, F1000, and Mendeley.

The endorsement system allows a scholar to recognize their contacts' skills and/or specializations. LinkedIn implemented this system in 2012, and ResearchGate launched "Skills" feature in May 2013. The endorsements to a scholar are often included in the scholar's profile to add credibility to the scholar. Although giving an endorsement does not require the permission from the scholar who is endorsed, current implementation of endorsement on the academic social web (such as LinkedIn and ResearchGate) does requires that the endorser and endorsee have a mutual relationship. In the case of RsearchGate, where the connections between scholars are based on a follower system, it requires the two parties of endorsement have to follow each other, which helps to establish some kind of checking mechanism in endorsement. Because LinkedIn has contact relationship, which is a mutual relationship, there is no need for such checking mechanism.

Table 2.7: Summary of key features on developing relationship among scholars

Function	Key Features	General Descriptions	Feature Examples
Developing Relationship with other peer researchers	Contact system	A feature supports two-way connection, where users can share their information through contact list or receive updates. Usually needs a permission from both parties.	LinkedIn, Mendeley (before March 2014)
	Follower system	A feature supports one-way connection, where the scholars who follow a user can receive the user's updates. Usually does not need a permission from the user.	Twitter, Mendeley (March 2014), RG, Google Scholar Citations
	Endorsement system	A feature allows scholars to recognize or get recognized peers' work skill or specialization. Could need or not need a permission.	LinkedIn, Research-Gate

Table 2.8: Summary of key features on grouping and co-production

Function	Key Features	General Descriptions	Feature Examples
Grouping and co-production	Mission-oriented co-production team	Feature that help academic users involved in a common task to achieve goals (such as discuss a working draft).	Academia.edu Sessions, Research Gate Project (discontinued), F1000's journal club (discontinued)
	Long-term interest community	Feature that supports users to form a group and share information, exchange resources, or seek discussions.	LinkedIn groups, Mendeley groups

2.2.2 GROUPING AND CO-PRODUCTION

Similar to their offline activities, scholars in the online academic social web often form communities and sub-communities. Kietzmann et al. [2011] stated that the grouping function "represents the extent to which users can form communities and sub-communities. The more 'social' a network becomes, the bigger the group of friends, followers, and contacts (p. 7)."

Depending on the purpose of grouping, groups on the academic social web can last for different length of time. In general, the groups can be classified into two types: mission-oriented co-production teams and long-term interest communities. Both of them can form communities for online scholarly collaboration.

Mission-oriented Co-production Teams. Scholars can form teams to perform many different tasks and achieve many different missions. Therefore, different academic social websites, based on their goals and interpretations of scholarly collaboration, have developed a variety of functions in this type.

1. *Academia.edu's Session.* A "session" on Academia.edu focuses on the mission of peer reviewing a document just uploaded by a scholar to Academia.edu. By default, Academia.edu will create a session and invites all mutual followers to comment on a scholar's uploaded work. Of course the scholar user can unchecked the "enable Session" button to stop the launch of a session. The document in the sessions is displayed by the Scribid viewer, and peer scholars can anchor his or her comments anywhere in the document, or just publish a general notice. A session usually lasts for three weeks. There are only few studies on Academia.edu's sessions, and it is criticized as been low awareness among the scholars on Academia.edu.

2. *ResearchGate's Project.* ResearchGate once rolled out a new feature called "Project" in May 2012, but it is no longer available as of June 2015. To the best of our knowledge based on few available documents, this feature allows scholars on ResearchGate to create a project and several "benches." In each bench, project members can share files and adds comments beneath a file.

3. *F1000's Journal Club (discontinued).* F1000's Journal Club is a mission-oriented service that features supports of face-to-face meetings. It provides features such as virtual scheduling using an online calendar, meeting description with the location, topics and the name of the meeting, advanced meeting document share, and meeting invitation to all potential attendees. The Journal Club on F1000 allows the task of meeting organization to be performed one integrated platform, rather than using multiple online tools such as Gmail, Google Docs, and Google Calendar. However, further investigation is required to see whether or not scholars are willing to embrace such integrated function. On the one hand, many Computer-Supported Cooperative Work (CSCW) studies praise integrated grouping tools for their productivity (e.g., one-stop shopping), but on the other hand, researchers seem pessimistically believe that users are creatures of habits and would be hesitate to abandon their already commonly used individual tools for a new integrated tool like F1000's Journal Club just for one type of tasks.

4. *Collaborative Real-time Editors.* Collaborative editors enable scholars to co-write documents in real-time so that the collaborative productivity can be improved Herrick [2009]. The collaborative editors have been implemented in many scholarly social websites, and the

most widely used ones include Google Docs and Hackpad Perkel [2014]. Taking Google Docs as an example, a collaborative writing tool usually has the following features:

- basic word processor functions such as formatting, image inserting, numbering, and bulleting text;
- basic highlight functions to any part of the document;
- attaching writing and editing to individual users, and providing mechanisms such as names or icons to direct access the users' editing;
- tracking changes (called revision history in Google Docs); and
- commenting.

Because scholars can co-edit documents in many different situations, collaborative real-time editors can be used in various steps in scholars' research cycles to leverage the benefits of collaboration.

Long-term Interest Community. Scholars often have long-term interests on certain research topics. Therefore, they can form online communities to share ideas and articles that they are interested in to discuss and read. For example, Mendeley Group allows users to start a long-term interest group, and it provides three types of groups:

- public groups that are publicly visible, can be searched in Mendeley's group list, and can be joined without any restriction;
- invite-only groups that are publicly visible, searchable, but can only be joined by an invitation or under permission; and
- private groups that are only visible to the members.

Scholars can engage into the groups as one of the two roles: either as a member who can contribute to the discussion or reading articles, or as a follower who can only observe the activities in the group without any explicit contribution of articles. However, both members and followers can annotate an article as a "Like" or make other types of comments on the group's wall. Other group contents include the entire publication list, the member list and the rules for interacting with other group members on the group's wall.

2.2.3   INFORMATION EXCHANGE

Scholarly information exchange is tightly connected with information and communication technologies. In the context of the academic social web, we classify information exchange into two categories: sharing research materials and resolve questions.

Sharing Research Products. Academic libraries and archives used to play primary roles in the management of accessing, preserving, and curating of scholarly materials, so sharing research

Table 2.9: Summary of key features on information exchange among scholars

Function	Key Features	General Descriptions	Feature Examples
Information exchange among scholars	Sharing research products	Feature that supports users to upload and share articles or research products.	Github, figshare, protocols.io, labfolder
	Resolving research questions	A social Q&A styled platform.	ResearchGate Q&A, Quora, Stack Overflow

products was mainly worked through them. However, first with digital libraries and more recently with the academic social web, individual scholars, intuitions, journal publishers, and professional associations are now jointly taking responsibilities for the management of scholarly materials, most of which are "born-digital materials."

Therefore, scholars can share their various research products online. Thanks to the advance of cloud storage and its user-friendly file management interface (such as meta tags extracting and drag-and-drop modules), sharing research products has become easier and more intuitive than before. Users can simply paste a link, or drag and drop a PDF file, and the system will help extract available information. Due to different types of research products that have been shared, there are many platforms allowing researchers to share their different research products. This includes:

- manuscripts (pre-prints): ResearchGate's open review;

- codes, scripts, software products: GitHub;

- datasets: figshare, /Mendeley Data, ResearchGate;

- reading lists/citations: Mendeley;

- figures or posters: figshare;

- presentation files: SlideShare; and

- research procedures/ methods: protocols.io.

Resolving Research Questions. Social question and answering (Q&A) provides a platform on which users can exchange information by asking and answering questions to other users [Harper et al., 2010]. Such Q&A platforms have been implemented in the academic social web too. For example, ResearchGate Q&A enables scholars to post questions for seeking information, or start an open discussion with other researchers [Goodwin et al., 2014]. Similar to general social Q&A sites such as Yahoo! Answers, academic social Q&A sites provide various incentive mechanisms

Table 2.10: Summary of key features on building conversation

Function	Key Features	General Descriptions	Feature Examples
Building Conversation	Remote video conferencing	Function that allows users at two or more locations to communicate by two-way video and audio transmissions.	Google Hangouts, Skype
	Instant message system	Feature that allows two or more users to send and receive real-time text.	Facebook, Google Hangouts
	Site mailbox	Feature that allows users to send asynchronized message on the social media site.	Twitter, Mendeley, ResearchGate, Academia.edu, LinkedIn, etc.

to encourage scholars to ask, answer, or comment questions within the community. However, academic social Q&A also has its own uniqueness. For example, askers in ResearchGate Q&A do not have to close their questions within a given period as these questions might be open-end research questions, and scholars in a question-answering thread do not have to vote for one best answer for there might not be single best answer.

Stack Exchange is another example academic Q&A platform. It has 144 sites so far (as of June 11, 2015), and each site covers a specific topic. Some famous sites include the well-known "Stack Overflow" (for programmers) and "Mathematics" (for math-related questions).

2.2.4   BUILDING CONVERSATIONS

When face-to-face meetings are not feasible, remote video conferencing tools such as Skype and Google Hangouts are effective alternatives for academic discussion. Instant messaging (a.k.a. two-way chat in Olson et al., 2000) such as Facebook messenger and Google Hangouts is commonly involved in remote discussion too, but it is unclear whether and to what extent this communication medium can impact academic information exchange, since these tools are designed for personal use. Synchronized message systems, such as the site mailboxes provided by academic social networking sites, are another type of medium for academic information exchange. The advantages of having on-site mailboxes include that the parties of email exchanges can easily know the identity of one another and that emails from on-site can be separate from personal mails. Many academic social sites, including Mendeley, ResearchGate, and Academia.edu, have on-site mailboxes.

2.3 MECHANISMS FOR ENGAGING GENERAL PUBLIC

The concept of public engagement is defined by the Higher Education Funding Council for England (HEFCE) as "specialists in higher education listen to, developing their understanding of, and interacting with non-specialists" (as cited in Weller [2011, p. 76]).

Traditionally, scholars' practice of public engagement can be demonstrated in several ways, including writing books with general interests and organizing student volunteer services [Weller, 2011]. However, the sharing functions of recent Web 2.0 tools allow concepts and ideas to spread quickly and widely, and these tools might require fewer costs for scholars to gain awareness from more general populations. Moreover, a crowd-funding platform provides a chance for scholars to receive physical or financial supports.

In this section, we discuss three kinds of mechanisms for scholars to interact with the general public.

Table 2.11: Summary of functional block for engaging general public

Mechanisms	General Descriptions	Examples
Crowdsourcing platforms	Platforms allow researchers to obtain needed content or get tasks resolved by outsourcing to a large group of people on the Internet.	Amazon Mechanical Turk
Crowdfunding platforms	Platforms allow researchers to receive financial assistance from the public.	Kickstarter, Indigogo, Experiment
Citizen science platforms	Citizen science projects try to engage the general public in gathering, processing, or analyzing scientic data in their academic projects. Citizen science online platform thus facilitates information exchange, data registering, and communication.	Texas invasives, eBird, Old Weather, Zooniverse

2.3.1 CROWDSOURCING PLATFORMS

Crowdsourcing refers to a recently emerged online and distributed problem-solving and production model [Brabham, 2008]. It was coined by Jeff Howe in his June 2006 *Wired* magazine article [Howe, 2006]. Crowdsourcing represents the act of taking a function or task used to perform within a particular institution to an online environment so that the function or the task can be completed by "an undefined (and generally large) network of people in the form of an open call" [Howe, 2006].

Due to the difference of crowdsourcing tasks, it is hard for researchers to categorize the relatively diverse set of crowdsourcing practices. Schenk and Guittard [2011] proposed a classification scheme that is useful in an analytical and an operational perspective. Their scheme used three aspects, namely, cognitive dimension of the tasks, nature of incentives, and benefits of crowdsourcing. Based on the nature of a crowdsourcing task, Howe [2006] and Schenk and Guittard [2011] classified crowdsourcing platforms into following categories.

1. *Implicit crowdsourcing*. In implicit crowdsourcing, users usually do not know they are contributing to a crowdsourcing project. A well-known example is reCAPTCHA, which asks people to solve CAPTCHAs (i.e., Completely Automated Public Turing test to tell Computers and Humans Apart) to prove they are really human rather than a bot. This input can meanwhile help digitize text such as *New York Times* Article Archive.

2. *Crowdsourcing idea game*. A well-known case is Google Image Labeler. In each round of the game, two randomly paired users are asked to label an image. If the two users give the same answer, then they move on to the next challenge. The matched answer is considered a good description of the image and will be used by Google to improve its image search service.

3. *Crowdsourced problem solving*. In crowdsourced problem solving, a requester can submit his or her own task and request for help from others. A well-known example is Amazon Mechanical Turk. Amazon Mechanical Turk (hereafter: MTurk) is a crowdsourcing platform, or marketplace, that allows individuals to coordinate the human intelligence to complete specific tasks.

4. *Prediction markets*. In the prediction market, investors from the crowd buy and sell futures related to some expected outcome such as the presidential election.

Although it was first developed as an innovative business model, crowdsourcing has been widely applied in various academic settings [Buecheler et al., 2010]. For example, Plenge et al. [2013] engaged a number of groups from academic institutions, private foundations, and for-profit companies to participate the Rheumatoid Arthritis Responder Challenge. Lease and Alonso [2012] invited people on Amazon Mechanic Turks to involve in evaluation of information retrieval algorithms. Lin et al. [2014] collected social tags from Amazon Mechanic Turks to annotate images in a museum, and Lu et al. [2015] studied people's health information intent in Yahoo Answers via crowdsourcing on content analysis.

2.3.2 CROWDFUNDING PLATFORMS

If crowdsourcing engage general public via their human power, another related concept, "crowdfunding," enables scholars to draw the money power from the public. Instead of soliciting external financing from a small group of sophisticated investors, crowdfunding raises financial support from a large number of people (the "crowd"), in which each individual provides a very small amount [Belleflamme et al., 2014]. General crowdfunding platforms, such as Kickstarter and In-diegogo, are used to support projects in all kinds of areas, not just scientific studies. However, Experiment (formerly Microryza) allows researchers to initiate a project on the site, to share the project description and budget overview in order to attract public awareness of the project. Similar to the management of other funded research projects, scholars on projects funded in Experiment need to keep updating their current research status, including having applied for the IRB or ar-rived at the field location. But unlike in Kickstarter and Indiegogo where sponsors often receive tangible items for a return, "backers" (i.e., citizen sponsors) in the Experiment projects will receive intangible credits such as getting recognized in the Acknowledgment sections.

2.3.3   CITIZEN SCIENCE PLATFORMS

Similar to the application of crowdsourcing in an academic setting, citizen science tries to engage then general public in gathering, processing or analyzing scientific data in their academic projects too [Bonney et al., 2009]. Therefore, citizen science includes crowdsourcing as one of its features, but crowdsourcing often engages individuals for a specific a task, and the individuals aim to get paid or be rewarded. Once the individuals receive their payment or reward, the relationship is usually over. In contrast, most citizen science projects aim for a longer and constant scientific participation from individuals.

Due to their diversity, it is difficult to classify citizen science platforms. Wiggins and Crow-ston [2011] proposed five "primary goals" for citizen science projects, which helps to classify citizen science platforms into five categories: education-oriented projects, conservation-oriented projects, investigation-oriented projects, action-oriented projects, and virtual-oriented projects.

However, we think that citizen science platforms are not just different at their goals. There-fore, we propose a classification schema with eight different facets, each of which has multiple degrees of values from the highest to the lowest (see Table 2.12). As a proof of concept, we propose a classification framework derived from a thorough evaluation of many citizen science projects (e.g., Texas Invasives, eBirds, Old Weather, Digital Fisher, CreekWatch, MoonZoo, The Quake-Catcher Network, etc.). The classification can be further refined by more reviewing citizen science projects at a larger scale.

We then organized citizen science platforms into four groups: community-based field work, observation network, virtual data processing, and participatory sensing/computing. As shown in Table 2.12, these four groups can be listed on a spectrum with all eight facets having their values move from the highest to the lowest along the spectrum. The two extremes of the spectrum are community-based field work and participatory sensing, while observation network and virtual data processing project locate in the corresponding position on the spectrum.

Community-based Field Work. On platforms for *community-based field work*, participants can expect to work in a physical place and perform multiple tasks from collecting data, analyzing it, drawing on a report. Moreover, some projects encourage participants to engage in a more complex decision-making process bonding with an environmental advocacy, such as recognizing,

Table 2.12: Summary of functional block for engaging the general public

	Community-based Field Work	Observation Network	Virtual Data Processing	Participatory Sensing/Computing	
Task Complexity	Higher	←		→	Lower
Acitivites Engaged in Research/Action	Multiple stages	←		→	Single stage (data gathering)
Individual Effort of a Single Input (e.g., one-time submission)	Higher	←		→	Lower
Training Workshop Required	More	←		→	Less
Threats to Internal Validity	Higher	←		→	Lower
Sense of Community	Higher	←		→	Lower
Social Ties with People in the Same Project	Stronger	←		→	Less
Participation Interval	Event-based or mission-oriented	←	any time	→	Ubiquitous

reporting invasive species, and then removing them. Therefore, before or during the projects, the participants are usually required to join a local workshop for training. Since local project leaders and participants might have a chance to meet and interact directly, we can consider that volunteers in this category might have stronger ties to the project. A local environment setting also strengthens the social bonding and volunteer's sense of community.

The Texas Invasives (Texasinvasives.org) is a citizen science project that tracks non-native invasive species in Texas. Their goal is to "protect Texas from the threat of invasive species" (Texas Invasives, n.d.). To achieve this goal, the Texas Invasives site not only provides informative description about identified invasive species for educational purposes, but also allows users to report encountered invasive species.

Observation Network. In the second group, *observation network*, the general public participants help the scientists to collect data from a physical environment by submitting data in their own device. Compared to the first group, volunteers in this group are not required to engage in multiple tasks across a research process. They mainly help scientists gathering data. Data they need to report usually contains location, a checklist, and some binary options such as presence or absence. As for the work environment, most volunteers can also complete tasks close to their local neighborhood, or during the way they walk home. Since there is less effort expected, local training workshops are seldom required either. Most of projects simply place training materials online.

The best-known platform for this category is eBird (`ebird.org`). Launched in 2002 by the Cornell Lab of Ornithology, in partnership with the Audubon Society, eBird is a real-time, online database which provides scientists with data about bird abundance and their geographical distribution.

There are several bird observation projects making use of eBird, such as FeederWatch (`feederwatch.org`) and Great Backyard Bird Count (hereafter: GBBC; `gbbc.birdcount.org`). These different projects have different themes and focus. GBBC is an annual four-day event every February that encourages participants to only spend 15 min on investigating their surrounding sky and the landscape. However, a contributor does not need to affiliate with a specific project: even there is no special project underway, a eBird user can always contribute bird watch data and submit them to the platform. The eBird also allows users to access any past list they contributed, and able to see other participants' effort.

Virtual Data Processing. Virtual data processing platforms are pretty much similar to Wiggins and Crowston's Virtual categorize. The most obvious common characteristic in this group is the working environment—all these platforms in a virtual setting. The leader scientists had already collected large scale of data themselves either from deep ocean, museums, or millions of cell slides. The reason that they rely on the power of crowds is because humans can process more complex and delicate information much better than computers. Because the tasks that the participants performing may require very less knowledge of a given domain and thus might not that interesting, many may confuse this type of citizen science projects with a general crowdsourcing task. The key of the success of this kind of citizen science platforms is to develop a sense of community among the participants. Particular platform supports include establishing community-based social support, introducing gaming features (e.g., Happy Match) or level-based honor systems (e.g., Old Weather and Digital Fisher) to motivate volunteers. However, even though we have seen more and more projects in this group, it is still a big challenge to recruit, motivate and retain participants in these platforms.

The old Weather (`oldweather.org`) is a well-known data processing platform. The ultimate research goal behind the Old Weather project is to study and model global climate through analyzing long-term temperature records in logbooks maintained by the crew. Led by Oxford University and the Met Office in UK, the Old Weather project was launched in 2010.

In Old Weather, volunteers read handwritings on the pages from the logbooks and report accurate measures (in handwritings), by which climate scientists can refine their model and study climate evolution. As we mentioned, keeping volunteer making contribution is an important key for running a citizen science project. The Old Weather project platform, therefore, maintains a community forum which has rich resources and lets scientists and volunteers share information. For example, volunteers share the stories that they read from the logbooks, asks peers to clarify some handwritings, etc. This online platform ensures that volunteers keep their incentive, sense of community, and productivity.

Participatory Sensing and Computing. Participatory sensing and computing platforms particularly emphasize the involvement of individuals in the process of sensing where they live. Except the location they perform the sensing task, there is less human judgment in this kind of project. People who collaborate with scientists only need to perform very few steps when collecting data. There is no need for reporting details sometimes: the participants just turn a sensor on.

For example, in the Project Quake-Catcher Network (`qcn.stanford.edu`), the sensor and the software installed in participants' personal computers will automatically report information to the research center when there is an earthquake. There is not too much space for a citizen to add their value on. Since there is much less effort and human involvement required than other kinds of citizen science projects, there are also less concern of motivation and incentives.

Overall, these four groups of citizen science platforms provide technical supports for scientists and volunteers to engage scholarly collaboration at different levels. The collaborations in community-based field work are usually at various tasks and across multiple research stages, which could include gathering data, writing reports, or even taking into an action. On the other side, the support to the collaboration in the participatory sensing platforms, such as the Quake-Catcher Network, would focus more on gathering accurate earthquake data because researchers need these data to build better models.

Following this observation, we can see that the technology supports in the community-based field work and observation network will usually include more educational training to the participants in order to control the validity of the outcomes of the collaboration. In contrary, virtual projects and sensing projects have less concern of validity and reliability because they reduce error by checking repeat data. For example, the Old Weather project, an online weather project by engaging volunteers to digitize log books, allows multiple users to digitize a same page in order to check the agreement. In terms of partnership, scholarly collaboration in the community-based field work platforms be a much stronger relationship than that in virtual environment or participant sensing projects.

Through our study of technology supports in citizen science projects, we further summarize the following features that would contribute to a successful online citizen science project:

- user-friendly protocols (e.g., website, mobile interface);

- training programs;

- application for submitting data;

- incentive-based systems;

- gaming features; and

- virtual community building work.

2.4   SUMMARY

In this chapter, we reviewed three technology functional blocks that support scholarly collaboration on the academic social web. The first functional block prepares scholars for their online research activities: (1) it supports researchers' day-to-day research tasks such as paper search and reference management; (2) it establishes scholars' online identities by creating online profiles; and (3) it gathers metrics reports for users. The second functional blocks either assists researchers to collaborate with peer researchers, such as finding collaborators and grouping. The third functional block bridges citizens and scholars through citizen science platforms.

After introducing several academics social network platforms, we leave it as an open question whether academics are comfortable with using features or technologies directly adapted from general social media platforms. For example, Mendeley's group post assembles Facebook's wall post, and ResearchGate adopts LinkedIn's endorsement system. On the other hand, features specially designed for academics have not gained much success so far. For example, F1000's JournalClub (which combines calendar, meeting scheduler, email, and slide sharing function) is no longer available. This might hint that researchers prefer a platform that integrates existing services to a platform that provides a new one-stop shopping service. We will have further discussion on this matter in Chapter 6.

In the next chapter, we will examine how social platforms can facilitate scholarly collaboration in each research stage, including conceptualization, data gathering, data analysis, and dissemination.

CHAPTER 3

Coupling Work for Social Scholarly Collaboration

3.1 OVERVIEW OF COUPLING WORK

Research collaboration, as Katz and Martin [1997] pointed out, is not just in multiple-authorship publications. Most collaborations often begin informally, and can take various forms in order to achieve "commitment to co-operate." This is why the nature of the work to be collaborated on is an important factor for studying scholarly collaboration [Olson et al., 2008]. In addition, collaborative research tasks are inherently knowledge-intensive, and interdisciplinary in nature [Anandarajan, 2010]. It is worth exploring how scholars engage in various research tasks throughout their research process.

Therefore, the discussion in this chapter aims to gain more insight on how scholars collaborate in research tasks. We will examine some nature of the collaborated work, but the main focus of our discussion is on "coupling works," a concept proposed in Olson et al. [2000]. In their work, coupling refers to "the extent and kind of communication required by the work" [Olson et al., 2000, p. 162]. We believe that concentrating on coupling work rather than work itself helps to capture the dynamic nature of a collaboration, as well as the collaboration parties' efforts on achieving the collaboration.

When multiple parties collaboratively complete a task, it is believed to be a success strategy to divide the task into modules and allocate the modules clearly among the parties, which enables different parties to work on the allocated modules in parallel [Olson et al., 2008, p. 79]. If this modularization can be relatively easily achieved for a task, we would state that the execution of the collaboration of the task does not require tight coupling [Olson et al., 2000] and thus the modules are reciprocal interdependent [Thompson, 2010].

Achieving loose coupling in work means demanding little unnecessary communication among parties. This is a feature that is very useful in online collaboration [Olson et al., 2008]. Thus, it is critical for scholarly collaboration on the social web too since the team created on the social web could be much looser than those in actual world. The modularization of the work can be achieved either by the nature of the work itself or by constantly define and refine the modules of the work.

This modularization idea was also mentioned by Nielsen [2012] in his discussion of collaborative patterns that help to achieve successful online collaboration. Besides modularization, he further identified "encouraging small contributions" and "developing a rich and well-structured information commons" as two other important criteria for successful online collaboration [Nielsen, 2012, p. 33]. These criteria can be used to evaluate whether certain tasks are suitable for online social scholarly collaboration.

Related to coupling work, the literature also discussed several other features. For example, if the work is clearly defined, and the goal and the scope of the work is unambiguous, it would lead to successful collaboration [Olson and Olson, 2013]. In addition, if the collaborators are already familiar with the work, and have developed a well-defined collaboration routine for the work, it would lead to successful collaboration too [Olson and Olson, 2013].

Due to the diversity of research work in different circumstances, scholars can perform many types of works on the academic social web. Some works might be suitable for collaboration online, whereas others might not appear in any online collaboration at all. Therefore, in order to help us examine the nature of the work in its context, we introduce research process as a way of organizing research tasks into categories. Here we assume that tasks performed in the same stage of the research process are more similar than other tasks that are in different stages. Particularly, our examination of the research tasks draws evidences from our discussion of the ready technology supports of academic social media sites reviewed in Chapter 2.

3.2   STAGES AND COLLABORATION IN RESEARCH PROCESS

Conducting a research work is a complex process that includes various actions. Most disciplines simplify the general research process as a sequential order which reflects the "journey" of the research [Malins and Gray, 2013]. However, scholars have indicated that "research is an iterative process of observation, rationalization, and validation," which is not necessarily a linear flow [Bhattacherjee, 2012, p. 20].

Based on their similarity and their focus, the actions in a research process can be roughly grouped into four stages in Table 3.1, according to Bhattacherjee [2012], Fraenkel [1993], as well as Hayes [2013]. We do acknowledge that these stages are not the only possible abstraction of the research process, and it might be more suitable to deductive and functionalistic in nature [Bhattacherjee, 2012, p. 20]. Furthermore, it is also not necessarily sequential without any feedback loop. However, our essential goal here is to use this relatively well-accepted model of research process as the framework to discuss whether or not certain types of actions in research process are suitable for online scholarly collaboration. In the remainder of Section 3.2, we will present in detail the stages and research actions in each stage.

3.2.1   COLLABORATION IN THE CONCEPTUALIZATION STAGE

The conceptualization stage contains two major actions, both of which can provide opportunities for scholars to collaborative. The first action is developing research topic and questions [Creswell, 2009]. A research topic is a set of specific questions about an interesting behavior, event, or phe-

Table 3.1: Research actions and stages

Stages	Research Actions
Conceptualization	Developing research topic and questions
	Literature review
Design	Selecting research paradigm
	Defining variables and samples
Execution	Measurement
	Data gathering/collecting
	Data analysis
Dissemination	Authoring
	Sharing and presentation

nomena that the scholars seek answers in the research [Bhattacherjee, 2012, p. 21]. It can emerge from individual thought exercises such as extensively reviewing the literature and developing from the scholar's practical experiences, or it can derive from talking to other researchers, which thus involves an implicit or explicit scholarly collaboration, respectively. The outcome of this action is to be able to describe the research topic concisely in a form of short description or a working title. At the same time, the identified topic is evaluated as to be researchable or not [Creswell, 2009, p. 2], during which the factors are considered include the suitability of the project for the time, resources, and availability of data; the relevance to personal interests and of interests to others; the innovation in the literature; and the contribution to the career goals. All these factors can be weighted alone or can consult with others through collaboration.

The second action is literature review, whose goals can include presenting results of similar studies, relating the present study to the ongoing dialogue in the literature, and providing a framework for comparing results of a study with other studies [Creswell, 2009, p. 45]. Therefore, literature review at least collaborates implicitly between the scholar and other scholars who produced the relevant studies. Scholars can also collaborate explicitly in reviewing literature where they could divide the review task by subtopics, time, or document types.

3.2.2   COLLABORATION IN THE DESIGN STAGE

After the conceptualization stage, a research project moves to the design stage, whose main actions involve the selection of right research methods. There are essentially three research paradigms: quantitative, qualitative, and mixed methods [Creswell, 2009]. Research paradigm helps scholars to define their research at a high level, and also enable scholars to select the right strategies of inquires which provide specific direction for procedures in research design. Examples of the strategies include experimental designs and surveys for quantitative approaches, ethnography, and grounded theory studies for qualitative approaches, and sequential or concurrent for mixed methods. Then at the third level, scholars utilize their understanding of the purpose of their research studies to decide the right methods for data collection, analysis and interpretation, which in all are called research methods. An example of research methods includes collecting attitude data both before and after an experimental treatment, and the data are analyzed using statistical procedures and hypothesis testing [Creswell, 2009, p. 16].

As shown above, the design stage is a complex process involving multiple layers of research knowledge. Because of the further separation of disciplines and expertise, scholars could find that they need collaborators in order to be equipped all the knowledge and skills needed for the research design stage. In this case, researchers need to identify collaborators and maintain collaboration relationships during the research process. Whether or not the right collaborators can be identified and maintained, and what are the collaborators' relevant skill set in the research project, would have significant impact to the research design and even the outcomes of the research project.

3.2.3   COLLABORATION IN THE EXECUTION STAGE

The execution stage of a research process often involves collecting and analyzing data based on the research methods constructed during the design stage. Although major design decisions have been decided at this stage, there could be specific issues related to this stage too. For example, a pilot testing could be conducted to examine more on the measures designed in the research. Another common issue is related to how the data can be collected directly from the fields or from the selected datasets available on the web [Bhattacherjee, 2012, Creswell, 2009].

Scholars engage various collaboration in the execution stage too. At those earlier stages of research process, scholars typically rely on personal relationship, but the collaboration among scholars at the execution stage is more concerned about task-levels and have production-oriented goals [Kraut et al., 1987]. For example, scholars have to explicitly communicate with their collaborators about the actions themselves in the context of data collection and data analysis, the reasons behind these actions and the outcomes of these actions. All these are related to the complex technical knowledge that must be shared among the collaborators [Kraut et al., 1987].

Besides sharing information, it is important for the collaborators to coordinate their activities at the execution stage too. Coordination is important in other stages too, but it is very critical at the execution stage because both data collection and data analysis are complex and expensive actions so that scholars want to make sure that all related activities get done and they are not done redundantly, and "that components of the work are handed off in a timely manner without impeding another's progress" [Kraut et al., 1987, p. 42].

3.2.4   COLLABORATION IN THE DISSEMINATION STAGE

Academia encourages at least implicit collaboration among scholars, so that there are strong incentives for scholars to write up their research achievements, then share and present to others.

Therefore, authoring and sharing/presenting research achievements are the two major activities in the dissemination stage.

Increasingly, research projects are conducted collaboratively among multiple scholars from the same or multiple discipline(s). Consequently, although writing is often viewed as a solitary process, scholars need to perform collaborative writing to turn their research results into formal communication products, such as journal articles, conference papers, reports, etc. [Neuwirth et al., 1990]. Before the wide usage of the academic social web, scholars used various means for writing collaboratively, including sending parts of the manuscripts via emails.

3.3   COUPLING ACADEMIC TASKS ON THE SOCIAL WEB

Scholars perform collaboration on social media for completing various academic tasks. Through studying over 2000 researchers, Nicholas and Rowlands [2011] found two important characteristics of the academic tasks performed collaboratively on social media. First, overall, the tasks performed collaboratively are very diverse and cover all the actions within the conceptualization stage to that within the dissemination stage. Second, the majority scholars as individuals often focus on conducting online collaboration on activities that are related to one or two specific research stages; only very few researchers engage collaboration on actions related to all stages [Nicholas and Rowlands, 2011].

In the remainder of this section, we discuss in detail the coupling work on the academic social web in each research stage.

3.3.1   COUPLING WORK IN THE DISSEMINATION STAGE ON THE SOCIAL WEB

Among the four research process stages presented in Section 3.2, activities in the dissemination stage are probably the most commonly performed on the academic social web [Gruzd et al., 2012]. According to an international survey conducted by University College London on nearly 2,000 scholars from more than 200 countries, among various uses of social media in their research workflow, social media was found most helpful during the dissemination of research findings. Not surprisingly, many academic social platforms are equipped with functions to support scholars for research dissemination.

This stage generally contains two tasks: content authoring and content sharing. Content authoring is a popular task on the academic social web. Nández and Borrego [2013] reported that 74.4% scholars they surveyed performed "document creation, edition and sharing" on the social web. Nicholas and Rowlands [2011] identified that collaborative authoring is one of the top three tasks performed by scholars. Through a content analysis on 126 blogs from a research blog aggregator ResearchBlogging.org, Shema et al. [2012] found that 84% of bloggers wrote their blogs as if writing academic papers using their real names, referencing other papers in a scholarly manner (e.g., referred to high-impact journals with proper citation styles), and blogged mostly about research in life sciences (39%) and behavioral sciences (i.e., psychology, psychiatry, neurosciences, 21%).

The other task in the dissemination stage is sharing and presenting results. In this case, blogging tools are being observed for many scholars to disseminate their results in their field and to the general public (e.g., Luzón, 2009, Nández and Borrego, 2013), and more recently microbloging tools such as Twitter are often used before and during academic conferences for advocating accepted papers (e.g., Gruzd et al., 2012, Ross et al., 2011).

With the help of social and web technology, scholarly collaboration outcomes have taken diverse forms as well. Through analyzing European scholars' web CVs. from astronomy and astrophysics, public health, environmental engineering, and philosophy, Kousha and Thelwall [2014] found that these web CVs. included blogs and social networking sites such as scholars' Mendeley profiles, LinkedIn profiles, and Facebook profiles. Furthermore, among the reported 2,700 cases, they found that various types of research products were listed on scholars' web CVs, which include document files, presentation files, statistic datasets, video files, image files, and audio files. This indicates that scholars are more open about taking advantage of the Web for sharing various types of their research achievements. On the account of research outcomes shared by scholars on the Web, Borgman [2007] further suggested that, just like books and journal articles, primary sources and research by-products—data, methodologies, tools, protocols, laboratory notebooks and the like—are parts of integrated formal research outputs for the present-day scholarly information communication system.

Despite the dramatic differences among research methods and research outcomes in different disciplines, dissemination on an academic social network is found to have very high usefulness across many disciplines. For example, Nicholas and Rowlands [2011] found that the two tasks of disseminating research results received the highest perceived usefulness among all tasks performed on the social web services (e.g., social networking, blogging, microbloging, and image/video sharing) across all four major disciplines they studied (i.e., arts, humanities, and social sciences; business and management; biosciences and health; and natural sciences, engineering and technology).

3.3.2   COUPLING WORK IN THE CONCEPTUALIZATION STAGE ON THE SOCIAL WEB

The conceptualization stage contains research topic identification and literature review as two actions. As stated in Section 3.2.1, both actions are among the top performed by scholars on the social web, and they often are perceived as most useful on multiple social web services. Nicholas and Rowlands [2011] found that the perceived usefulness score of performing research topic identification on the academic social web was constantly among the top in all four major disciplines they studied. Over 75% of the scholars in Nández and Borrego [2013]'s study stated that they performed literature review on the academic social web.

Developing research topics and questions involves creating, thinking, exploring, conceptu-alizing, and brainstorming. Furthermore, creativity emerges out of activities that involve interac-tions among individuals and their sociocultural context. Social media, particularly academic social sites, provide rich content for exploring research questions and supporting scholarly writing [Gu and Widén-Wulff, 2011]. Maron et al. [2009] interviewed faculty members in 46 colleges about the digital resources they use for their research works. In total 206 unique digital resources faculty members identified, discussion and blogs received attention comparing with e-journal and ency-clopedias. When a scholar is exploring a new or unfamiliar topic, we can imagine that academic social platforms can serve as rich repositories for information exchange and materials sharing.

The academic social web also appears to serve a brainstorming space for idea sharing and for new knowledge creation [Panahi et al., 2013]. For example, the academic social web provides different tools to support informal communication among scholars: Blogs, Wiki, academic social Q&A, collaborative authoring tools, all of which provide powerful features for scholars working together. Scholars have been found to utilize these tools for their actions related to conceptualizing their research projects. For example, Kirkup [2010] as well as [Gruzd et al., 2011] found that scholars used social web services to explore unasked questions in an informal atmosphere, and to discuss issues in an open, public format, both of which are important for identifying research topic. Another example is that Bonetta [2007] found that scholars often read blogs authored by peers as a means to keep up with current research and issues in their field.

3.3.3   COUPLING WORK IN THE DESIGN STAGE ON THE SOCIAL WEB

Scholars commonly perform collaborative tasks related to the design stage on the social web. Gruzd et al. [2011] found that scholars often used the social web to strengthen existing collab-oration relationships, as well as to form new ones with scholars of similar interests and research areas. With its global reach, the social web is found to facilitate international or interdisciplinary collaboration, or build up collaboration with people outside academia as well [Collins and Hide, 2010, Nicholas and Rowlands, 2011].

When trying to identify and maintain collaborative relationships on the social web, scholars heavily rely on existing communication tools and technologies. Commonly utilized tools include instant messages, web conferencing tools, and web scheduling tools. Web conferencing was found to be used by almost three-fourth of scholars in Nández and Borrego [2013]'s study. In the same study, scheduling services on the social web seem to be perceived as very useful for scholars too.

In comparison, we do not observe much discussion on the connection between research method selection and the social web. No matter if the studies were about various academic tasks performed on social web services (e.g., Nández and Borrego, 2013) or the studies about scholars' perceived usefulness of social web services in research workflow (e.g., Nicholas and Rowlands, 2011), we have not found any direct mentioning of the research paradigm/method selection task. However, we do acknowledge that the discussion of paradigm/method selection could happen in research meetings or conferencings, which means that we would not see explicit support from the social web to such tasks.

3.3.4   COUPLING WORK IN THE EXECUTION STAGE ON THE SOCIAL WEB

As stated in Section 3.2.3, the execution stage mainly focuses on the task of collecting research data and analyzing the data. Therefore, the first coupling work in this stage is on using academic social network for collecting data.

In certain research studies that involve human subjects, recruiting participants is an important sub-task for collecting research data collection. In this case, (academic) social web services, with their strong capabilities of connecting a wide range of people, can provide great help. Researchers have found generic social networking services such as Facebook and Craigslist can be used to recruit participants which transcend barriers such as "physical distance, transportation, and limited time and financial resources" [Yuan et al., 2014, para 30]. Gray et al. [2013] illustrated several examples of using social media to efficiently recruit human participants (they called patient) for providing research data collection. Jeng et al. [2015] also found that academic social networking services, such as Mendeley, can help those researchers who would like to study "junior scholars' information behaviors or run a survey on a wide range of online scholars." From the point view of recruiting human participants, we can see the similarity to a related concept called crowdsourcing. Amazon Mechanic Turks is the most famous platform for supporting crowdsourcing that has increased applications to scholars' research activities in various disciplines [Buettner, 2015, Goodchild and Glennon, 2010]. However, crowdsourcing has the critical issues of lacking control of the data quality and the right types of participants [Allahbakhsh et al., 2013].

Another interesting development in the execution stage is that researchers are increasingly interested in viewing the academic social web as the source for providing a real, large quantity of research data, making academic social websites themselves the actual research platforms on which to perform data collection [Gray et al., 2013]. Jeng et al. [2015] followed the same idea, and utilized data available on Mendeley to study scholars' collaboration behaviors.

In certain disciplines, not just the data but also the process of running experiments is important knowledge to be shared. For example, experiment protocols for collecting data play an important role in bio-health fields, therefore, bio-health scholars utilized social platform such as "protocol.io" to share the experiment protocols. However we also noticed that this practice of online sharing of experiment protocols has relatively low awareness in the community, probably because it is a quite new idea and platform. In addition, it has not been adopted by other similar disciplines too.

In comparison, a data analysis task receives less support on the academic social web. Crowdsourcing provides some form of collaboration for data analysis but it is on rather simple, easily divided analysis tasks [Allahbakhsh et al., 2013]. Fortunately, there is increasing awareness of this issue, and we do see some new online services for supporting such tasks. No matter what, scholars are aware of the importance of the social web in their data collection and data analysis tasks. For example, Nicholas and Rowlands [2011] found that scholars in natural sciences, engineering, and technology, as well as biosciences and health, all think social networking services, blogging, microblogging, and social tagging/bookmarking can play an important role in their data collection and analysis tasks.

However, not all tasks in all fields are suitable for collaboration online. Nielsen [2012, p. 75] points out that "in fields where a shared praxis is available" collaborative intelligence can scale, and thus provide qualitative shift. But for fields without shared praxis, online tools do not work. Shared praxis refers to a body of knowledge and techniques shared by all the participants or in a community.

3.4   FACTORS AFFECTING SCHOLARLY COLLABORATION TASKS ON THE SOCIAL WEB

Besides tasks in the stages of a research process, researchers have found other important factors that can affect the coupling work on the social web as well [Nicholas and Rowlands, 2011].

The first factor comes from different social platforms. For example, Veletsianos and Kimmons [2012] found that, due to the limitation of number of words in a microblog, scholars often use microblogging as the means for various informing functions. This includes sharing short announce information (e.g., *"[Speaker] is discussing education and technology at [institution name]: [URL]"*), drawing attention to professional endeavors (e.g., *"Visit my colleague's [name] new blog and leave her a comment [URL]"*), requesting assistance or offering suggestions (e.g., *"user name : Here is an example [URL] user. I can also send my course schedule if you need it."*), and informing others of their current activities (e.g., *"Heading to [#conference name]: [URL to map pinpointing current location]"*).

The second one is discipline influence. For example, Computer and Information Science domains might have earlier adoption of online information techniques [Jiang et al., 2013]. Scholars in Earth Sciences, Environmental Sciences, and Physics are among the top disciplines to engage scholarly collaborations online, whereas scholars in Business and Management, Health Sciences and Biosciences, the Arts and Humanities are significantly less likely to use social media tools in their research [Hagstrom, 1965]. This is to some degree consistent with other studies on research collaboration, where applied research and interdisciplinary areas call for more collaboration because they require a wider range of skills.

The third factor lies in the scholars' own characteristics. Nicholas and Rowlands [2011] found that scholars' three characteristics are particularly relevant here. The first characteristic is the age of the scholars. Scholars who are younger than 35 are significantly more likely to use social media than the older group (82.6% vs. 75.7%). The second one is where the collaborators of the scholars are. Scholars who work with collaborators in different institutions have a significantly higher chance to use social media than the scholars who work with colleagues in the same department, in their own research, or work with colleagues across the same institution. The third characteristic is the seniority of the scholars in a research team. Senior scholars perhaps are more "likely to be involved in project negations or preparing presentations" so their usage of social media might be more around "collaborative authoring tools for sharing and editing documents, scheduling and meeting tools, and conferencing," whereas junior scholars' collaboration tasks are more involving in microblogging, social tagging, and bookmarking.

3.5   SUMMARY

The research tasks performed by scholars can greatly affect their collaborations online, therefore the focus of this chapter examined the tasks performed by scholars in their research process. Using a cascade model for research process, we examined the scholarly collaboration tasks performed at each stage on the academic social web. The discussions in this chapter showed that scholars' research tasks can be diverse, and the collaboration tasks can happen at all stages of the whole research process, although activities in certain stages happen more often than others.

In addition, there are several factors affecting scholarly collaboration tasks on the social web, which include platform influence, discipline influence and scholars' own characteristics.

Overall, it seems that it is important for research work to be modularized so that the collaboration can "divide the problem its attacking into tasks that can be done by single individuals" [Nielsen, 2012, p. 50]. Because not all the research tasks can be easily modularized, therefore scholars who involved often need to made "a conscious commitment to be modular, and then relentlessly followed through on that commitment" [Nielsen, 2012, p. 51].

CHAPTER 4

Common Ground for Social Scholarly Collaboration

4.1 COMMON GROUND IN COLLABORATION

When people collaborate with each other there is a need to establish a shared understanding [Ansell and Gash, 2007]. This shared understanding is often called common ground, and it can be on one or many different aspects of the collaboration. The common ground originates from people's shared context, such as mutual knowledge, similar training, or common beliefs, and it can be presented by the way of communication and languages. For example, a common ground can be found in a public lecture. The speaker needs to incorporate common ground with the audiences by considering suitable examples and avoiding unfamiliar jargon.

Common ground can be established based on prior interactions or from immersion in a shared environment. For example, Kraut et al. [2002] found that users who were previously unacquainted can develop social and work relationships in chat rooms because the repeated experience in the shared environment, chartrooms, establishes common ground. It is worth mentioning that, when there is no direct prior experience to draw from, people tend to assume the existence of common ground "if they know they are members of the same group or have experienced the same event" [Kraut et al., 2002, p. 147].

Establishing common ground is an iterative process, in which people exchange information about "what they do or do not understand" (Clark and Wilkes-Gibbs, 1986, as cited in Kraut et al., 2002). Clark and Wilkes-Gibbs [1986] called this iterative process grounding. It is not difficult to imagine that communication techniques play an important role in the process of grounding, which facilitate information exchange among people. As pointed out by Clark and Brennan [1991] and discussed in Chapter 2 of this book, different communication media provide different communication functionalities, resources, and incur different costs and efforts. Therefore, the discussion of grounding has to be closely connected with the available environment where the collaboration is happening.

Olson et al. [2008] identified three key factors contributing to the grounding process, which are (1) previous collaboration experience, (2) common knowledge, and (3) shared common beliefs or assumptions. Following Olson's model, our discussion of building common ground is around these three factors in the context of the academic social web.

Besides, being different to collaboration in the physical world (where the collaboration partners can physically collaborate or near to each other), potential collaborators on the academic social web may not have prior collaboration experience nor can establish shared understanding through face-to-face meetings. Consequently, when scholars on the academic social web try to establish common ground for their collaboration, they probably more often rely on the online profiles of other scholars for grounding process. This is why we will first talk about the important roles of online profiles in building common ground before discussing Olsen's three key factors.

4.2   IMPORTANT ROLES OF SCHOLARS' ONLINE PROFILES

As stated in Chapter 2, academic social web platforms are featured in profile building for scholars. The profiles provide information about the scholars' academic affiliations and positions, their research interests, expertise levels, geographic locations, and many other things. The profiles also include various indicators about the scholars' research achievements such as publications, funded projects, etc. All these indicators help to evaluate the expertise, seniority, and reputation of the scholars.

Information in the profiles can then be used by scholars for seeking collaborations. For example, Schleyer et al. [2012, 2008] proposed a Digital Vita system as a prototypical design for scholars to seek online collaborators. Digital Vita builds scholars' profile around their academic Curriculum Vitae (CV), and utilizes CV to provide the most up-to-date and comprehensive online description about a scholar's accomplishments and activities. Around such profile information, Digital Vita then provides four main functions: maintaining, formatting, and semi-automated updating of biographical information; searching for researchers; building and maintaining social networks; and managing document flow.

Discussions in Chapter 2 stated that, with the help of the academic social web, it is much easier for scholars to collaborate with wide range of researchers, not only in the same domain but also interdisciplinary. This, however, causes problems in building common ground on the academic social web because there is much less information available within the online profiles of individual scholars, and at the same time, there is much higher communication costs involved for grounding process. Therefore, there are studies seeking to discover more offline information about individual scholars that might not be available on the academic social web [Becerra-Fernandez, 2006]. Examples of such offline information includes resumes [Aleman-Meza et al., 2007], publications [Wang et al., 2013], blogs [Balog et al., 2009], microblog postings [Bozzon, 2013], other footprints such as Q&A posts in other generic online community sites [Bouguessa et al., 2008], etc. Once such extra information is available, scholars' online profiles are enriched for building common ground.

Since there are still relative few studies on scholars' finding of online collaborators, we acknowledge that the discussion in this section lean more toward expert finding systems which automatically locate online potential collaborators rather than studies on scholars' online behaviors. However, we still believe using implications that we learned from these expert finding systems is valid because these automatic systems are designed to locate potential online collaborators as well. In addition, the theories and hypotheses in studies of expert finding systems have been widely tested and applied.

4.3   COLLABORATION BEHAVIORS FOR RECORDING PAST EXPERIENCE

When partners in a collaboration reach a common ground, individuals are able to not only capture each other's contributions in the collaboration, but also reveal the potential limitations to each partner. [Olson et al., 2000]. During the collaboration, scholars are looking for collaborators who can establish a working relationship. Therefore, particularly during the grounding process, the specific task or problem, although important, is probably secondary to forming and maintaining the relationship [Schleyer et al., 2012].

As stated in the previous section, collaboration on the academic social web can happen among scholars who have prior collaboration, or often can establish among those who just started their collaboration for the first time. Therefore, our discussion here first examines the situation where collaborators have prior experience, and then review the one without.

Scholars' past collaboration experience can appear in various tasks performed inside or outside of online academic social web. For example, scholars can use email exchanges for discussing a research idea [Ogata et al., 2001], or collaboratively writing articles that are collected in online databases such as DBLP and Citeseer [Li et al., 2007, Marshal, 2008]. hese two activities would not be directly captured by the academic social web. In contrast, scholars can explicitly identify their prior collaborators and social ties on the academic social web [Yang and Chen, 2008]. Consequently, some researchers, e.g., McDonald and Ackerman [2000], performed formal and informal interviews to discover scholars prior collaboration experience so that such information can be reveal for online collaboration. The Digital Vita system, as another example, blends two strategies, allowing scholars to specify collaborative relationships explicitly through "colleague requests" (equivalent to "friend requests" in Facebook) [Schleyer et al., 2008] while also deriving implicit ties such as co-authorship and shared department membership from CVs.

Another important issue is how prior collaboration experience, since it is essential knowledge for online collaboration, can be represented. For this, we think that the SWAT system provides a solution [Braghin et al., 2012]. SWAT represents the past experience as a history graph, on which individual scholars on specific expertise areas are recorded. Then such information is combined with online profiles and the social graph that captures the colleagues and friend relationships, help to provide a comprehensive information for online collaborator finding. The data used in SWAT include DBLP. Academia.edu, ACM DL, IEEE Xplore, Springer DL, and CiteSeers. SWAT's approach is based on Anandarajan [2010]'s long-term collaboration study on research collaboration in teams, although Taramasco's work was not directly on the line academic social web.

When there is no past experience, scholars, in order to build up common ground, then need to simulate past collaboration experience based on certain assumptions. For example, Pavlov and

Ichise [2007] developed link prediction algorithms to identify potential collaboration opportunities using the structural information in co-authorship networks. Another idea is a Facebook application called MEDLINE Publications (MP) [Bedrick and Sittig, 2008]. The system uses the PubMed database to automatically create user-customizable lists of publications so that a rudimentary recommendation algorithm can be developed to identify other users with similar publication profiles, thus to simulate co-authorship relationship that resembles prior collaboration relationship.

Schleyer et al. [2012] mentioned that scholars on the academic social web sometimes even try to use face-to-face communication to establish some kind of initial contacts for building up prior experience because face-to-face interaction seems to produce the highest trust among unfamiliar collaborators [Moore et al., 1999]. If face-to-face opportunities are absent, chat sessions and exchange of personal information can also help to overcome limited availability of information [Zheng, 2002].

4.4   COLLABORATIVE BEHAVIORS FOR BUILDING SHARED KNOWLEDGE

Although prior collaborative experience plays important role in building common ground, scholars in grounding process do not solely reply on the memory of past experience. They can utilize shared knowledge to interpret each other's statements. Once such shared knowledge can make sense, scholars are able to proceed for further collaboration. For example, the articles co-authored by the collaboration partners can be seen as an example of extracted common knowledge. Another example is that scholars in Mendeley Groups collaboratively contribute articles relevant to the focus of the groups so that the collection thus becomes the shared knowledge of the group [Jeng et al., 2015].

Therefore, taking Mendeley's Group function as an example, scholars can build shared knowledge with several different characteristics. First, the shared knowledge can be available to the partners in the collaboration only. For example, Mendeley support private groups where only accepted members of the private groups can see the content created by the group members. In this case, although such knowledge is shared, it is not accessible by outsiders. The benefit of the shared knowledge thus is only to facilitate these scholars' future collaboration.

Second, scholars can also make their shared knowledge open to others. For example, in contrast to private Mendeley groups, many Mendeley groups make all the written records in their groups, including their article collections, open to other scholars. Many owners of these open Mendeley groups, through carefully crafted statement about the purpose of the groups, actively encourage other scholars to join their groups so that a more collaborative relationship can be constructed [Jeng et al., 2015]. Studies show that those statements and the openness of the groups contributed greatly to the healthy development of these online collaboration relationships.

The outcome of building shared knowledge does not have to be published articles or other forms of research products. Sometimes, certain types of collaboration can help to record shared knowledge as well. For example, answers to an academic question or a thread of discussion around a research problem can both be invaluable information for future reference. This kind of representation of shared knowledge fits Van House [2004]'s view that "knowledge is always situated in a place, time, conditions, practices, and understanding" [Borgman, 2015, p. 39]. Based on this view, there are many social question and answers sites such as Yahoo! Answers and Stack Overflow, as well as academic online discussion services such as ResearchGate's discussion place.

Third, although many scholars only aim to build shared knowledge among their collaborators or potential collaborators within certain disciplines, some researchers look at the knowledge sharing as an ecological complex system: the concept of knowledge infrastructure, which can be seen as the further development of information infrastructure on the Internet [Borgman, 2015]. Knowledge infrastructure is defined as "robust networks of people, artifacts, and institutions that generate, share, and maintain specific knowledge about the human the natural worlds" [Edwards, 2015, p. 17]. The assumption is that such knowledge infrastructure will help to attach individual shared knowledge among collaborated scholars into the globally shared networks so that all other scholars on the networks can understand such knowledge too, which enables much broader shared understanding and thus much broader collaborations. When shared knowledge is constructed merely for the involved collaborators, as long as the collaborators can understand the representation, it is not critical on what format or coding the shared knowledge is represented.

An even broader examination of building shared knowledge might be needed in the knowledge sharing cycle [Huysman and de Witt, 2003, p. 30]. In this cycle, individual knowledge can be externalized to be shared knowledge, which then can be objectified to be organizational knowledge. Organizational knowledge then can be internalized to be individual knowledge. Organizational knowledge, shared knowledge, and individual knowledge all combined together to be in innovation knowledge creation.

When shared knowledge is constructed merely for the involved collaborators, as long as the collaborators can understand the representation, it is not critical on what format or coding the shared knowledge is represented. However, as soon as the shared knowledge aims to be understood by other scholars in order to enable wider collaboration, there are two critical problems to be resolved.

The first problem is how to let scholars from different disciplines use the same terminologies to refer to the same concepts. Knowledge representation experts think that controlled terminologies and ontology are valuable here [Perez and Benjamins, 1999]. For example, in discussion about Digital Vita, Schleyer et al. [2012] talked about the benefits of controlled terminologies can bring for sharing knowledge broadly, which include enabling cross-disciplinary searches, supporting identification of synonyms and related terms, and facilitating automatic discovery of otherwise undetected similarities between scholars. Liu et al. [2004] moved even further by proposing a Resource Description Framework (RDF) that combines a domain ontology with semantically rich information to represent knowledge.

The second problem is that the shared knowledge would contain too much information if the common ground is built among many potential collaborators, particularly on common knowledge. [Blair, 2010]. In such a situation, scholars need supports from automatic recommendation systems to filter through the vast shared knowledge in order to identify possible collaborators [Lee et al., 2010]. For example, Lee et al. [2010] proposed OntoFrame S3, a semantic Web-based academic research information portal, to enable automatic discovery of potential collaborators. Cameron et al. [2007] integrated semantic annotation with FOAF to determine scholars' expertise across various areas of computer science. However, although certain automatic algorithms and systems have been demonstrated to be useful in particular contexts, it is still a difficult challenge to develop an automatic collaborator system [Schleyer et al., 2012].

Borgman [2015] pointed out that the shared knowledge in collaboration could also include the tactic knowledge. The similar idea was also suggested earlier by other researchers (e.g., Ackerman et al., 2003). However, how to extract and represent such knowledge, compared to the relative static domain knowledge, is an even less known problem. Researchers only recognize that it is constant changing with "multiple parties negotiate how data are understood across disciplines, domains, and over time" [Borgman, 2015, p. 33].

4.5   COLLABORATIVE BEHAVIORS FOR SHARING COMMON BELIEFS AND ASSUMPTIONS IN MANAGEMENT

Researchers believe that collaboration is often formed through a process rather than a particular event [Kraut et al., 2002]. During this grounding process, besides task-related activities, collaborators also perform relationships-related activities, of which the essential one is to determine whether potential collaborators are acceptable partners. This activity can been seen as a compatibility assessment [Schleyer et al., 2008], which includes checking personality, work style, and other factors [Beaver, 2001].

Olson et al. [2008] mentioned that one of the key factors in building common ground is to identify shared common beliefs and assumptions. We think that this factor is relevant to compatibility assessment, which can be developed through prior experience but would not be represented in the shared knowledge.

In the academic social web, it might be difficult to observe scholars' common belief and assumptions. However, like Casciaro and Lobo [2005, 2008] pointed out, social matching is an important factor besides domain expertise. For example, when junior researchers look for their potential collaborators, they would consider whether or not the collaborators are socially close to them as either friends, or friends of friends. This maybe be viewed as some kind of substitution of sharing common beliefs and assumptions.

Terveen and McDonald [2005] mentioned another substitution of common beliefs and assumptions. They found that personal characteristics must be taken into account during the grounding process. They suggested that information about personality, friendliness, character, trustworthiness, sense of humor, and work style may be relevant here.

The third issue related to common beliefs and assumptions can derive from the importance of tactic knowledge. Hinds and Pfeffer [2003] mentioned the usefulness of tactic knowledge obtained through collaboration, and how such information, besides domain knowledge, can play in further collaboration. However, it is much more difficult to extract tactic knowledge embedded in a particular situation or environment, and therefore how scholars learn and share tactic knowledge still deserves further studies.

4.6   SUMMARY

Our discussion in this chapter focused on building common ground. As stated, scholars' online profiles enable much wide range of collaboration. Therefore, online invisibility becomes an important issue for scholars on the academic social web. Just as web services do not exist if nobody knows the services, scholars who are invisible online will increasingly have the same problem. Fortunately, it is much cheaper and easier for scholars to build up connections and shared knowledge, so as to maintain visibility to avoid negative Metthew effect.

Building common ground enables scholars to collaborate. However, increasingly broader collaboration also makes it harder for scholars to precisely locate potential collaborators among vast available candidates. Automatic recommendation systems and services thus become a useful solution. The concept of knowledge infrastructure in this case also plays an important role for deepening and growing shared knowledge and common ground. Of course, "A collaboration seeker's desire for comprehensive information needs to be balanced with potential collaborators' requirements for privacy and access control" [DiMico and Millen, 2007, Schleyer et al., 2012].

CHAPTER 5

Collaboration Readiness for Social Scholarly Collaboration

5.1 FACTORS AFFECTING COLLABORATION READINESS

Collaboration readiness evaluates individuals' specific factors that can facilitate team collaboration [Olson and Olson, 2013]. The specific factors can be stated as being related to the following three questions.

- Is there is a common goal between collaborators?

- Can participants trust each other to be reliable to work with?

- Are there are motivations for collaborators?

We will convert the discussions about goals and motivations over using the academic social web using related works on three groups: scholars' own characteristics, scholars' motivations, and the incentive mechanisms. We think that scholars can identify whether collaborators share the same goals or trustworthiness by looking at the collaborators' characteristics, and the incentive mechanism can encourage sharing the same goals or generating motivations for collaboration.

However, first, we need to discuss more about two closely related terms—motivation and incentive. According to Reeve [2014, p. 9], motivation is "an internal processes that give behavior its energy (implying the behavior has a strength), direction (implying the behavior has a purpose), and persistence (implying the endurance)." In this matter, the direction implies that the behavior has a purpose. Incentive means "an environmental event that attracts or repels a person toward an action" [Reeve, 2014, p. 136]. However, the incentive do not directly cause the behavior; instead, the incentives act as a "situational cue that signal the likelihoods." Therefore, once an incentive is not very effective, it decreases the likelihood of people's motivation.

Human behavior is complex, and what causes certain behaviors are of interest to many scholars who study motivations. According to The SAGE Glossary of the Social and Behavioral Sciences [Sullivan, 2009, p. 333], "theoretical models of motivation attempt to explain why individuals choose to engage in a particular activity." Previous efforts from scholars have shown that external events, job characteristics, personality, and prior life experience can affect people's behaviors and engagement in social activities [Kanfer et al., 2000, Latham and Pinder, 2005].

Self-Determination Theory (SDT) was developed by Deci and Ryan [2011], and has been discussed, applied, and refined by scholars all over the world. In SDT, people are moved by "extrinsic motivation:" external factors such as environmental incentives (e.g., rewards, promotion) and consequences (e.g., reputations, reviews, scores) [Reeve, 2014, p. 134]. On the other hand, people are also motivated by "intrinsic motivations:" by one's interests (e.g., for fun), psychological needs (e.g., inherent satisfaction or sense of belongingness), and personal curiosities. SDT has undergone public scrutiny since its conception and has been tested and applied to the field of knowledge sharing. Since the distinction of intrinsic motivation from extrinsic motivation, SDT can help discover the most critical motives behind scholars' collaboration and sharing behaviors: to examine whether scholars are motivated extrinsically by the increase in citation counts, or simply by the sense of achievement for sharing great research.

The Theory of Planned Behavior (TPB) is another theory raised frequently in the context of the use of social media [Mathieson, 1991]. For example, Gagné [2009] presented a conceptual model of knowledge-sharing motivation, which combines the SDT with the TPB. TPB concludes that "attitudes toward the behavior, subjective norms with respect to the behavior, and perceived control over the behavior are usually found to predict behavioral intentions with a high degree of accuracy" [Ajzen, 1991, p. 206]. Behavioral intentions can further be used to predict the actual behavior.

In Ajzen's TPB [1991], the first determinant of behavioral intention is people's attitudes toward the behavior. This refers to the extent "which a person has a favorable or unfavorable evaluation or appraisal of the behavior in question" (p. 188). Another conceptual factor is subjective norms regarding the behavior, including normative beliefs and subjective norms, which refer to "perceived social pressure to perform or not to perform the behavior" (p. 188). The third determinant of behavioral intention is perceived behavioral control over the behavior. This can be understood as a predictor that refers to people's perception of the "ease or difficulty of performing the behavior" (p. 188). Ajzen's TPB provides a theoretical basis for many scholars interested in humans' motivations for social media use.

Other than SDT and TPB, some scholars adopted the bottom-up approaches to collect the possible motives for academics to join or participate online communities and social media Thij [2007] came up with six categories of motivations when studying people joining an online group: social contact, information, financial or material benefits, support, interaction or discussion, and construction of self-identity. Butler et al. [2003] identified the concept of "perceived benefits" of participating in online communities as motivation, elaborating four types of motives: information benefit, visibility benefit, social benefit, and altruistic benefit.

Scholars have observed that professors as well as students use social media for various purposes, including personal communication, information sharing, and professional connections [Chen and Bryer, 2012, Tiryakioglu, 2011].

In Section 5.3, we will apply the concepts of extrinsic and intrinsic motivation and social media to systematically review the extrinsic and intrinsic motivations of the academic social web.

5.2   INFLUENCES BY SCHOLARS' OWN CHARACTERISTICS

No matter whether it is in face-to-face communication or interacting in an online environment, academic collaboration is a relationship among scholars. Scholars' individual characteristics become a critical factor that we would like to discuss in this chapter. Our review of the scholars' own characteristics focuses on the demographics of scholars who use social media, including general social media (e.g., Facebook) and academic social networks (e.g., ResearchGate or Mendeley), scholars' disciplinary culture, and finally their academic capitals. We further discuss if these factors, related to individual characteristics, play important roles regarding scholars' collaborations.

5.2.1   DEMOGRAPHICS

In the following, we discuss the demographics of academic users on social media, including general platforms and specialized platforms for scholars (e.g., ResearchGate and Mendeley).

In 2010, CIBER surveyed nearly 2,000 scholars from 215 countries and reported how these scholars leveraged social media in their research workflow [Rowlands et al., 2011]. Although the CIBER report does not provide detailed demographics of the participants, it shows that earth science, environmental sciences, and physics are the top three communities that utilize social media. Moreover, for all disciplines, there are at least 70% of participants answered that they use social media in research. Scholars also found that the natural scientists such as earth science, geological sciences, and physics are the keenest users on social web [Hicks and Sinkinson, 2015].

As for academic social web platforms, several studies have confirmed that the majority of users in the academic social web are junior scholars [Jeng et al., 2015, Jiang et al., 2013]. For example, Jeng et al. [2015]'s survey showed that the average age of Mendeley users was 35 years old and 64% of them were male. These results on gender distribution are consistent with Thelwall and Kousha [2014]'s work on Academia.edu. Furthermore, Thelwall and Kousha [2014] stated that even though female users have dominant presence in generic social networking sites such as Twitter, Facebook, and Instagram, the ratio between male and female users in the academic social web is approximately 64/35.

Table 5.1 compares the demographical parameters of online scholars collected by existing survey studies. The existing studies mainly utilized two categories of data collection methods: online questionnaire and profile collecting. Online questionnaires allow scholars to collect detailed personal information such as age and gender. On the other hand, profile collecting (i.e., extracting existing online profiles) is more suitable for collecting a larger sample.

All these studies were performed on multiple academic social websites, and the overall outcomes indicate that scholars who use academic social media are predominantly those early-careered scholars such as Ph.D. students [Hicks and Sinkinson, 2015, Jeng et al., 2015].

In the following, we will specifically discuss these scholars (who use the academic social web) with respect to their disciplinary aspect and academic capitals.

Table 5.1: Demographic parameters in prior studies on academic social platforms

Studies	Platforms	Sample Descriptions	Sample Size (N)	Data Sources	Demographic Parameters
Jeng et al. (2015)	Mendeley	Large group members or audience	146	Online questionaire	Gender, disciplines, age, position
Jeng et al. (2015); Jiang et al. (2013)	Mendeley	All users with available profile	7,366	Profile collecting	Disciplines
Thelwall and Kousha (2014)	Academia.edu	Users with the tag of philosophy	3,186	Profile collecting	Discipline (philosophy), gender, position
Elsayed (2015)	ResearchGate	Arab scholars in six research universities	315	Online questionaire	Institutions, age, position (academic rank), disciplines
Ortega (2015)	ResearchGate, Mendeley, Academia.edu, and Google Scholar	CSIC scholars in Spain	6132 profiles	Profile collecting	Disciplines, RG score,the average citations of each scholar.
Hicks and Sinkinson (2015)	Mendeley	Mendeley users in CU-Boulder campus	68 respondents	Online questionaire	Disciplines, (academic rank)
Mendeley Global Research report (2012)	Mendeley	ALL users on Mendeley (2 million as of 2012)	—	Internal data analysis	

5.2.2   DISCIPLINES

Traditionally, discipline culture is considered an important factor influencing scholars' collaborative behaviors. For example, Guimerà et al. [2005] compared the collaboration culture in four disciplines (including social psychology, economics, ecology, and astronomy) and found that more scholars involved in collaboration in astronomy over time than in ecology, social psychology, and economics. More recently, studies indicate such discipline differences as well. Mendeley's official report (2012) announced that the top five lager user groups in Mendeley are bio-medicine (31%), natural science (physical, chemistry, earth science, etc.) (16%), engineering (13%), and computer and information science (10%). This is later confirmed by other studies stating that the largest discipline groups in ResearchGate and Mendeley are biological science, medicine, computer science, and engineering [Elsayed, 2015, Jiang et al., 2013].

Other than the community composition, the behavior on the academic social web might be different as well. Holmberg and Thelwall [2014] indicated that the disciplinary difference can appear as the content that those scholars post on Twitter. For example, astrophysics scholars on Twitter tend to have more direct conversations than other disciplines where tweets might be more about links (e.g., in economics), or simply retweet others' posts (e.g., in biochemistry). Jeng et al. [2015], on the contrary, did find a statistical difference across disciplinary groups, by their motivation to use the Mendeley.

Although previous work showed most users were from STEM communities, Jeng et al. [2015] revealed that there is an increase in the user base from social science and humanities. According to Jeng et al. [2015], social science scholars might adopt the service slightly later than science users. However, Jeng et al.'s research suggests users in the social sciences might be potential users for Mendeley in particular.

Institution and geographical distribution. Scholars also studied the institutional and geographical distributions of academic social media users. A strong correlation was found between high-profile institutions on ResearchGate and the world renowned institutions. Thelwall and Kousha [2015] found that the institutional rankings are associated with several altmetrics on Researchgate. For example, the RG scores, paper download counts, and views of a profiles are positively correlated with the university ranking. Thelwall and Kousha [2015]'s investigation also pointed out that the national composition of ResearchGate is mostly concentrated around few countries including the U.S., India, U.K., and Germany.

5.3   EXTRINSIC AND INTRINSIC MOTIVATIONS OF SOCIAL SCHOLARLY COLLABORATIONS

5.3.1   EXTRINSIC MOTIVATIONS

Extrinsic motivations can be defined as motivations that come from external sources. The literature has identified three major types of extrinsic motivations that encourage scholars to participate in collaboration on the academic social web: gaining tangible impacts, gaining endorsements, and gathering resources.

Gaining Visibility and Impacts (e.g., citations, altmetrics). Gaining visibility and awareness is an important motivation in a social networking environment. Establishing a personal presence with increased visibility, scholars receive positive and significant rewards in terms of salary, reputation, and positions [Leahey, 2007]. Traditionally, scholars gain visibility by scholarly publishing. Citation-based bibliometric methods have been widely used based on scholarly publishing as a measure to evaluate scholars for hiring, tenure, funding, promoting, or other rewards and recognition [Borgman, 2007, Piwowar et al., 2007].

Today, scholars have more options to gain visibility for their works on various platforms thanks to a new way of analyzing scholarly impact indices (the so-called "altmetrics.") Altmetrics, contrary to using citations for measuring scholarly impact, examines the counts of scholars' various behaviors on the (academic) social web. Instances of data sources may come from social media included blogs, Mendeley readership counts, or Twitter mentions. Recent studies found that some altmetrics are correlated with the citations, which normally take years to accumulate [Thelwall et al., 2013, Zahedi et al., 2014]. Furthermore, we also see scholars engaging in online discussions and ASNS group activities, and increasingly such activities are considered as impacts of the scholars' academic activities too (such as the contribution to RG score in ResearchGate).

Gaining Resources (e.g., free dataset or publication access). Participating online communities not only can increase visibility and citation but also gain additional resources. Prior studies suggested that satisfying their informational needs could be another motivation for scholars to participate in online communities [Lampe et al., 2010]. People with information needs can participate in online communities either for acquiring information or for actively getting answers to solve their own problems [Porter, 2004]. Given such information needs of users, several social media websites design a "give-and-take" mechanism in which users could unlock more features or gather more resources when they keep on participating or contributing more content. For example, Pixabay (pixaby.com) is a photo-sharing community, and all newly registered Pixabay users can freely download others' photos legally after uploading some photos and granting others to download these photos without restrictions.

Viewing the whole academic social web as a repository, it is not difficult to imagine that academic scholars join an online community in order to gather teaching materials, research materials, or peers' suggestions that have research and pedagogical value [Veletsianos and Kimmons, 2012]. For example, ResearchGate's registered users are able to access other scholars' self-archiving full-texts and datasets.

Gaining Endorsements. In addition to the research outcome, social platforms can also be used to attract funding and social endorsement, as we discussed in Chapter 2. For example, researchers nowadays can raise research funding by running crowdfunding campaign on fundraising sites such as Walacea, Petridish, and Experiment. Researchers can also obtain virtual endorsements (i.e., recommendations from co-workers) on sites such as LinkedIn and ResearchGate. Such social recommendation can have a positive impact on personal branding.

5.3.2 INTRINSIC MOTIVATIONS

Intrinsic motivations can be defined as motivations that are inherently driven or out of enjoyments. The literature has discussed three major types of intrinsic motivations for scholars to participate in the academic social web: enlarging academic networking and ensuring research openness and transparency.

Enlarge Academic Networking. Through participating online communities, academic users can expand their professional network, and thus ultimately increase the opportunities to interact with their potential collaborators. The possible activities associated with it including communication, connection, or finding like-minded people [Jeng et al., 2015]. As with other online communities, social media become platforms that can gather academic people with similar research interests. Through participating the community, users are able to build their social ties and personal networks. For example, similar to the Facebook's group function, Mendeley Groups display a list of group members and allow users in the same group to connect to others right a way. However, Jeng et al. [2015, p. 900] observed that comparing with using research features, Mendeley users in general are "lack of socialization," indicting that "sharing expertise online might be challenged by difficulties conveying their knowledge or understanding to others."

Ensuring Research Openness and Transparency. Existing research found that scholars are motivated to help each other voluntarily in the real world [Kogan and Hanney, 2000]. Such an altruistic action is also recognizable in the virtual world [Lampel and Bhalla, 2007]. For example, Jeng et al. [2015] found that the altruistic motivation (i.e., provide more information to others) was one of the most important reasons for users to join more groups on Mendeley.

Research openness and transparency is another intrinsic motivations for scholars on ResearchGate to share their research outcomes [Elsayed, 2015]. Scholars on ResearchGate also believe that staying in the academic social web can thus "foster openness to the views and attitudes of scholars" and "increase awareness of the importance of sharing knowledge with other scholars" [Elsayed, 2015, p. 7].

5.4   INFLUENCES OF INCENTIVES FOR SOCIAL SCHOLARLY COLLABORATION

5.4.1   INCENTIVES ON ACADEMIC SOCIAL PLATFORMS

Incentive can be understood as an extrinsic drive that motivates people toward a certain behavior [Bernstein, 2013].

As the top business mission of most social media websites is getting more users and keeping current users, these sites often provide incentive mechanisms to stimulate users' contribution to content and resources, thereby later building a sustainable online community. According to Vassileva [2005], "a powerful incentive mechanism has to offer rewards for different types of users, and their preferred types and styles of contributions [Vassileva, 2005, p. 3]." That is, because of the diversity of incentives, the same incentive might not work on different users. Hence, before deploying an incentive program, a website should assess the demographics and activities of its users on the site.

Although little work has been done to study the incentives for the academic social web, we can draw experience from the rich literature on the incentive mechanisms of generic social media or online communities.

We discuss the different goals toward the incentive designs, and they can broadly be classified into two types: *encouraging contributions* and *encouraging user commitments* [Kraut et al., 2012]. "Contributions" are directly related to users' willingness to generate contents, help the community to grow, whereas "commitments" help keep users in the community.

Encourage Contributions. Social websites have been found to provide strong incentives to encourage their users to contribute more content because users' interaction and discussion are centered around content (or social objects). This happens to generic social sites such as Youtube for videos, Instagram for photos, Foursquare for check-ins in, Yahoo! Answers for Q&A, and academic social site such as Mendeley for references, and Academia.edu for articles.

The most common incentive mechanism for encouraging contributions on these social sites is the honor system, usually through a gamification feature: users can accumulate more "points," "scores," or "badges" and advance to higher levels. Well-known example includes Waze levels in Waze, badging system in Foursquare, and level-up system in Yahoo! Answers. Along with the users advancing to the next level, the website may unlock new features or privileges or promote users to a different status (which stands out from normal users). Note that such a level-based or badging system can also encourage user commitment at the same time because users would like to stick around the sites and see their status level up.

Another common incentive mechanism to encourage user contributions is via social bonds because people usually respond to the request "if they come from others who are familiar to them, similar to them" [Kraut et al., 2012, p. 33]. Therefore, it is essential for a site to increase its user base. Both monetary and virtual benefits (e.g., free storage spaces or coupons) can be provided when existing users bringing their friends. Dropbox Space Race is a well-known example. Participants in higher education draw their peers to register Dropbox accounts and won the free storage space based on their overall rankings.

Encourage Commitments. As for commitments, the goal is still to enroll more users or ensure the sustained productivity of contents, which can be achieved via common incentive mechanisms that deepen the quality of content or participation.

To enhance the quality of website content, several sites actively recruit and acquire endorsements from experts and celebrities. They recruit well-known users or hire editors to ensure high quality content. For example, Tumblr hires experienced journalists and editors to produce high quality post. Google+ created celebrity projects and "fans will now jump on the Google+ platform to keep tabs on their favorite stars. [Martin, 2001, para 2]."

Besides the main content (e.g., videos on Youtube), supplementary content (e.g., user comments on Youtube) is also important for growing user commitments. To encourage users to participate in providing feedback (such as user rating, user comments, feedback), websites often provide virtual currency or participation points as incentives [Vassileva, 2012]. Sometimes the incentives can be implicit. For example, Rashid et al. [2006] found that users are more willing to provide ratings if they found that their contributions can improve the community (as cited in Harper, 2007). To cultivate the sense of community, some websites allow users to create their own sub-groups. For example, a Facebook Page is a sub-community that makes users stick to the website.

As the sites aiming to support academic scholars and their communities, academic social websites share most ideas about incentive mechanism presented above, but they also have their own twists.

Table 5.2: Incentive models and academic social web platforms

Platforms	Goals	Instances	Incentive's Models
ResearchGate	Stimulate user's participation	RG score	Participation points and reputation-based system
Mendeley	Gaining more users	Advisor Program, Sub-group function	• Honor badge and virtual perks • Mendeley Groups
F1000	Gaining more users	F1000 scholars (well-known faculty)	Celebrity endorsements

As shown in Table 5.2, ResearchGate, Mendeley, and F1000 are the three academic social websites that have clear incentive mechanisms. ResearchGate employs an incentive mechanism called RG score. RG score is not only a participation point system but also a "metric that measures scientific reputation" that based on a scholar's research [*ResearchGate*, n.d., para 1]. When users contribute to the contents to ResearchGate, such as adding a bibliography, full-text articles, datasets, or answering other scholars' questions, these activities can count toward the scholar's RG Score. Other than content contribution, adding journal articles with Web of Science (WOS)'s impact factors will also help accumulate RG Score. Similar to Cheng and Vassileva [2005] where they found users will log in more frequently to check their points and status, RG Score can encourage scholars' contribution as well as their commitment because it can stimulate scholars to contribute contents and at the same time ensure that the scholars who wish to accumulate RG score will keep visiting the site.

Instead of adopting the participation point system, existing Mendeley's incentive mechanism is called Mendeley advisor program and Group function. Mendeley Advisor is an honor program for which users can apply. The obligation of a Mendeley Advisor is spread by word of mouth, holding workshops, and sharing teaching materials about Mendeley. In return, Mendeley offers the advisor premium features such as more storage space and more quotas of creating private groups. Mendeley advisors also receive badges in their profiles. Beside the advisor program, Mendeley's Group function can be seen as a sub-community. (Discussion about sub-community can be found in Chapter 2 and Section 4.4.)

F1000 employs a different strategy to that of ResearchGate and Mendeley. According to F1000's website, the site invites "Heads of Faculty" who are "world-renowned scientists and clinicians" in different domains. However, the effect of such a strategy is still unknown.

5.4.2   LACK OF INCENTIVES OUTSIDE OF THE SOCIAL WEB

Despite active support with various incentive for scholarly collaboration on the academic social web, one big hurdle that prevent scholars from being ready to collaborate on the academic social network is the lack of incentives outside of these sites—the scholars' endeavors on the academic social web are not widely recognized and lack rewards toward their academic careers.

The most significant problem is that scholars' endeavors on the academic social web are not currently recognized by most of the research institutions [Weller, 2011], especially in the tenure and promotion review process [Gruzd et al., 2011, p. 2]. The lack of official support and encouragement from scholars' institutions is thus a major disincentive for scholars to spend extra time on managing their scholarly activities on social media.

There are two possible reasons behind this problem. The first one is related to the still unclear relationship between functions of traditional scholarly communication and that on the academic social web. Researchers who study scholarly activities on the academic social web do recognize that these activities are part of the research process, but it is unclear how important those activities are.

The second reason is that the activities scholars conducting on the academic social web are often viewed as earning "micro-credits," which are difficult to be recognized and thus in turn to be assigned with proper rewards [Weller, 2011]. In other words, there are too many activities to know the importance of each. It seems that scholarly activities using these new social technologies are beneficial to research, but researchers are yet to accept them as the essential functions of scholarly communication.

However, there is still room for optimism. According to Piwowar [2013], National Science Foundation (NSF) now asks the PIs of projects to list the significant research "products" rather than "publications" in their biographical sketch. This policy helps to encourage scholars and their institutions to think "acceptable products" are not just articles, but any "citable and accessible" academic outcomes, which include but not limited to "publications, data sets, software, patents, and copyrights" [NSF, 2013]. Although it still has to travel long way to reach the state that preprints, semi-results, presentation slides, or datasets on the academic social web such as

ResearchGate or figshare can be recognized as useful research products, this shift to value a wider range of research products may be a significant step.

SUMMARY

In this chapter, we reviewed recent literature and further discussed about how scholars build on their collaboration readiness—that is, prepare themselves to be ready for a collaboration on social web. In the context of the social web, scholars can use their online profiles to disclose and discover potential collaborators. However, different disciplines, geographical area, and academic capitals may lead to different composition or behaviors in on the academic social web.

We then talked about the motivations that are driven by external rewards or recognition (extrinsic), and intrinsic ones such as altruistic motivations or the belief of open research. We reviewed a variety of current incentive mechanisms on the academic social web; however, the effectiveness of them remain unknown. Future work is much needed to examine if these incentive mechanisms truly work for raising scholars' willingness to collaboration and the commitments to stay on a community.

To date, we concluded that scholars' social media footprints and contributions are not strongly tied with with the faculty reviewing process or career promotion. Nevertheless, the NSF's new policy on grant proposal allows PIs to list out all related research products. This change thus can be considered as a significant shift which recognized a wider range of research outcome, and perhaps value credits and contributions on the social web some day.

CHAPTER 6

Discussions and Conclusions

Scholarly collaboration is important, and it is increasingly more important on the academic social web. This book divides the problems into four parts using Olson's scientific collaboration model, including technology readiness, coupling work, building common ground, and collaboration readiness. We expect to establish interesting directions for further research, and to stimulate more discussions on scholarly collaboration on social web.

For technology readiness, we show that several academic social platforms have been developed, and although many of them have their unique features, most of them aim to support important aspects of scholarly collaboration on the social web.

For coupling work, this book examines the tasks performed by scholars on the academic social web, and indicates that activities in all stages of scholars' research process have their corresponding supports on the academic social web, particularly the dissemination stage.

Our review on building common ground shows that scholars indeed perform various activities to facilitate their collaboration online, which include establishing online identities, enabling recording past experience, building shared knowledge, and building common beliefs and assumptions.

Finally, the review of collaboration readiness establishes again the demographic influence to the collaboration online, the impacts of scholars' extrinsic and intrinsic motivations for online collaboration, and the incentive designs for encouraging scholars' collaboration.

6.1 IMPLICATIONS

Based on the discussions in previous chapters, we will highlight several insights and limitations of the work presented in this book. They include the potential challenges and opportunities regarding the rise of academic social media platforms, the preservation and reuse of content generated by researchers' online activities, and the role of "management, planning and decision making," which is the fifth factor of successful collaboration mentioned by Olson.

6.1.1 SCHOLARLY COLLABORATION ACTIVITIES

Although it is still at its infancy, the academic social web does play an increasingly important role in supporting scholars' research work. Particularly, various forms of collaboration are thriving on the academic social web. This book shows that all scholarly activities have their appearance on the academic social web; however, the levels of popularity on one or across different platforms are quite different.

On one side, there are various supports for scholars to establish their identities and profiles on the academic social web. As the basis of online collaborating when scholars might not have previous collaboration experience, this is very useful. Some scholars only provide an alias online, but more and more scholars use their true names in these online platforms. In addition, more and more online profiles contain academic products that the scholar produced in their scholarly work so that the collections of products not only become part of the online profiles but also the online knowledge repository of the discipline. Therefore, their online profiles are increasingly the extension of the scholars' academic profiles for research. Accordingly, scholars also use online profiles, including reputation scores to identify potential collaborators. The online repository also enable scholars to perform dissemination of their research products, which speed up the scholarly information exchange, and also help both implicit collaboration as well as explicit collaboration.

However, at the same time, we also see some research activities have less appearance on the academic social web, which thus hinder the collaboration around these activities. For example, only in some part of the academic social web with community question and answering functions can we see some discussions about the potential research topics, research methods and possible approaches of analyzing research data. Beyond that, we have not seen any social platform explicitly support collaborations on information exchange with research methods, nor repositories of tools and procedures for conducting data analysis.

Our reviews also show that, besides research activities, some online users on the academic social web are mostly ignoring some social networking features such as friend making.

Perhaps these missing research activities and social engagement are somewhat more difficult than those already supported activities. For example, the discussion of potential cutting edge research topics would require selfless contributions from leading scholars in the filed, who are often too busy to do such things and also there is no strong incentive mechanism on the social web as well as in the discipline to support such activities. The similar situation exists to tools for analyzing data, but is probably better since increasingly the filed is recognizing the scholarly contribution of researchers to design and develop such tools. Maybe a wide range of incentive mechanisms is needed to recognize scholars online collaboration activities [Piwowar, 2013].

Eventually, we might have to look at academic collaboration as some form of commercial activities. Similar to the exchange of goods, we exchange scholarly information for gaining the information that we want. Based on the information exchanged, we build up collaboration relationship. However, that requires direct exchange of information, which like direct exchange goods, requires that both parties see the value of the exchange. The invention of currency resolves this problem, and enables the currency to be used as the intermediary for the exchange so that there is no requirement that the exchange parties have to all agree with the values of the goods. Maybe the academic social web is the primitive markets that early people developed for exchanging goods. Here scholars start to use open market (the academic social web) to exchange research products (papers, tools, datasets, ideas, methods, and so on). We used to collaborate in a way of face-to-face, or we need to exchange information. ICT helps us to overcome the time and space, but what about discipline and norms? For the further development of the exchange, some form of currency will be needed in order to enable more flexible exchange of scholarly products.

To some degree, online incentives on the academic social web is acting like primitive currency with limited functions. Right now, the academic social web offers a new opportunity as a kind of "online, sharable currency." Researchers can share and contribute their research products, ideas, and experience to the Web. Later, when individuals need to gather resources from others, they know where to find them. The Web becomes a huge repository. This give and take mechanism becomes an indirect collaboration. However, further mechanisms are needed that can exist and act beyond the academic social web so that broader scope of scholarly collaboration can be supported and facilitated.

Perhaps this indicates that the academic social web might not be the ultimate platform for support scholars' collaborations. As a complex research process, scholarly activities and scholarly collaboration require the availability of relevant knowledge and the mechanism to query and manipulate those knowledge. Therefore, a final support to scholarly collaboration might be the newly envisioned knowledge infrastructure.

6.1.2   ACADEMIC SOCIAL WEB PLATFORMS

Although the majority of attentions are still on generic social websites such as Facebook and Twitter, academic social website are increasingly popular among scholars. As the review in Chapter 2 shown, academic social websites are increasingly specialized to support academic scholars' activities, which including making presence (Section 2.1) and conducting collaboration (Sections 2.2 and 2.3).

However, there is also increasing confusion on the academic social web. One such confusion is that there are too many academic social platforms available. For example, our review in Chapter 2 mentioned Mendeley, Academia.edu, ResarchGate, F1000, Research4life.org, LinkedIn, figshare, etc. At the same time, we have seen many newly added platforms such as MethodsX, Brainly, Mendeley Data, and so on. While the existing platforms are still in the development stage, many successors have emerged for competition. All existing and new platform make scholars confused on which platform(s) to use, and cause segmentation among scholars or disciplines that actually need some form of shared platform for information exchange and collaboration. Maybe this just means that the academic social web is not mature enough to consolidate so that there isn't a "killer" platform that is very necessary or desirable for majority scholars in all disciplines? Or, does this mean that scholars haven't fully understood what they want?

Could we actually have been asking a wrong question? Maybe there will not be one academic social platform that can dominate the whole space. What scholars actually need in this networked participatory scholarship is a whole new knowledge infrastructure that includes many people, knowledge, and technologies [Edwards et al., 2013]. Each academic social platform or even the whole academic social web is just one module that aims to fulfill one particular academic function or scholarly primitive. Therefore, should we think about the academic social web in a bigger and more complex process, so that every existing and new academic social platform can be examined for its functionalities and maybe repurpose the functionalities for more modularized design in a complex process?

However, scholars also follow the human nature that tends to stick to the things that they are familiar with. This causes problems to new platforms as well as repurposed platforms. For example, in Chapter 2 we discussed the failure of F1000's Journal Clubs. Journal Clubs integrated functions that are similar to Google Calendar, Gmail, Doodle (a meet-up scheduling tool), and document sharing features. But scholars would rather stick to the services that they got used to (i.e., those Google services), and Journal Club failed quickly. This probably shows that we might not need an integrate of system that covers all aspects of online scholarly collaboration. The full support actually comes out from smartly and seamlessly combining existing tools that scholars already use in their daily research work and online communication.

Nevertheless, looking back at the architecture development of digital libraries, we do see a trend of open architecture and modularization of components and corresponding technologies for digital libraries [Suleman and Fox, 2001]. Therefore, maybe the focus of further development of the academic social web should not be on individual platforms anymore. The focus should be on the basic functions that all academic platforms should support, and therefore modularizes the development of the functions for the academic social web.

Thomas Friedman tells us that the world is flat. Through the academic social web, we indeed see that the academic world is getting flatter with the help of academic social web. Scholars from all the world, including those from Africa, Latin America, and India, are actively participating online collaboration in ResearchGate, Mendeley, and other platforms [Jeng et al., 2016], so that knowledge and information exchange are acting much faster than before.

6.1.3　CONTENT MANAGEMENT AND REUSE ON THE ACADEMIC SOCIAL WEB

Through this book, we increasingly realize that more and more academic information is exchanged on the academic social web. Studying such information helps us to gain insights on scholarly information exchange on the academic social web. At the same time, such information can be viewed as scholarly data that should be managed for archiving and reuse. Therefore, inspired by ideas studied in current research data management we discuss the following insights to the creation, interaction, preservation, and reuse of ASNS contents.

Content Creation. As the academic social web is different to generic social platforms in terms of their user types and the scholarly content, the academic social web needs better support in content creation in order to support scholarly information exchange. Our review of scholarly collaboration showed that some scholars have difficulties to engage online scholarly collaboration because they do not know much about activities happening within the platform. We think that the clarity and quality of organized scholarly information on the academic social web would significantly improve the usages of the academic social web by scholars. One possible tool is to integrate certain classification schemes with or without social tags to enable scholars to label or classify their questions based on their intentions, targeted audience, or even preferred sources.

Content Interaction. In order to more effectively and efficiently take advantage of valuable content on the academic social web, we think that a better interface is needed for presenting scholarly information. For example, academic information often contains a variety of important metadata information that could include URLs, the title of an article, or even a few lines for the abstract. Such metadata information can be extracted, classified, and visualized as a separate pane or integrated part of the social web interface. When a scholar looks at the information on the platform, he/she would be able to scan through all potentially useful resources regarding to the scholarly discussion, as well as navigate through them to different academic information.

Content Preservation. The long-term preservation of and access to research outcomes has become important and trending in data intensive science. We have seen libraries paying increasing attention to social media data. For example, the Library of Congress started to acquire public tweets on Twitter since March 2006. However, we have not seen preserving scholarly content on the academic social web being considered. We think that the information on the academic social web is important in terms of its content and in terms of being the underlying data for studying scholarly behaviors on the academic social web. Therefore, it is important to think how such scholarly information can be systematically preserved for future scholars.

Content Reuse. Scholarly online discussions often contain a large amount of useful knowledge for those that did not participate in the original discussions. Studying such scholarly content can enable other scholars to enrich the relevant topic discussed in the information exchange or such information can be used to study scholarly behaviors, or it can be collected as datasets for building automatic tools. This is a promising direction with numerous potential applications. For example, researchers can reuse this scholarly content as a corpus and apply machine learning and text mining techniques for automated classification and analysis. The results can inspire applications such as understanding the trend in each discipline or monitoring the common needs in different disciplines.

6.2   LIMITATIONS

Our book follows Olson et al.'s model in 2001, which contains only four factors. However, their updated 2008 model added one more factor called "management, planning, and decision making" [Olson et al., 2008]. We did not include this fifth factor in this book because we have not observed discussions about scholarly collaboration in the academic social web that is related to management, planning and decision making. Perhaps this is another indicator that the academic social web is still at it infancy, not all activities related to online scholarly collaboration are supported. It is therefore interesting to see how activities related to such factors can be implemented and supported in the future academic social web.

6.3 CONCLUSIONS

Just like Borgman [2007, p. 1] pointed out that the "Internet is now an integral component of academic life," The academic social web is part of a broader academic infrastructure, too. With the help of a complete infrastructure, scholars are increasingly collaborating with each other on the Web, regardless of time and space limitations. Despite the various limitations of the academic social web, scholarship in the digital age receives further boosts from these platforms to move into higher accelerations.

Bibliography

Ackerman, M. S., Pipek, V., and Wulf, V. (2003). *Sharing Expertise: Beyond Knowledge Management*. Cambridge, MA: The MIT Press. 52

Ajzen, I. (1991). The theory of planned behavior. *Organizational Behavior and Human Decision Processes*, 50(2), 179–211. DOI: 10.1016/0749-5978(91)90020-t. 56

Aleman-Meza, B., Bojārs, U., Boley, H., Breslin, J. G., Mochol, M., Nixon, L. J. B., Polleres, A., and Zhdanova, A. V. (2007). Combining RDF Vocabularies for Expert Finding. *Science*, 4519, 235–250. DOI: 10.1007/978-3-540-72667-8_18. 48

Allahbakhsh, M., Benatallah, B., Ignjatovic, A., Motahari-Nezhad, H. R., Bertino, E., and Dustdar, S. (2013). Quality control in crowdsourcing systems: Issues and directions. *IEEE Internet Computing*, (2), 76–81. DOI: 10.1109/mic.2013.20. 44

Altmetric.com. (2015). *What data sources does altmetric track?* Retrieved from `https://help.altmetric.com/support/solutions/articles/6000060968-what-data-sources-does-altmetric-track-`. 17

Anandarajan, M. (2010). *e-Research collaboration: Theory, Techniques and Challenges*. Springer Science & Business Media. 37, 49

Andersen, P. (2007). *What is Web 2.0?: Ideas, Technologies and Implications for Education*. (Vol. 1) (No. 1). JISC Bristol, UK. 5

Ansell, C. and Gash, A. (2007). Collaborative governance in theory and practice. *Journal of Public Administration Research and Theory*, 18(4), 543–571. DOI: 10.1093/jopart/mum032. 47

Balog, K., Azzopardi, L., and de Rijke, M. (2009). A language modeling framework for expert finding. *Information Processing and Management*, 45(1), 1–19. DOI: 10.1016/j.ipm.2008.06.003. 48

Bar-Ilan, J. (2012). JASIST@ mendeley. In *Acm Web Science Conference 2012 Workshop*. Retrieved from `http://altmetrics.org/altmetrics12/bar-ilan/` 14

Bar-Ilan, J., Haustein, S., Peters, I., Priem, J., Shema, H., and Terliesner, J. (2012). Beyond citations: Scholars' visibility on the social web. In *Proceedings of 17th International Conference on Science and Technology Indicators*, (Vol. 52900, pp. 98–109). Retrieved from `http://arxiv.org/abs/1205.5611`. 18

Beaver, D. D. (2001). Reflection on scientific collaboration (and its study): past, present, and future. *Scientometrics*, 52, 365–377. 52

Becerra-Fernandez, I. (2006). Searching for experts on the Web: A review of contemporary expertise locator systems. *ACM Transactions on Internet Technology (TOIT)*, 6(4), 333–355. DOI: 10.1145/1183463.1183464. 48

Bedrick, S. D. and Sittig, D. F. (2008). A scientific collaboration tool built on the facebook platform. In *Amia Annual Symposium Proceedings*, (Vol. 2008, p. 41). 50

Belleflamme, P., Lambert, T., and Schwienbacher, A. (2014). Crowdfunding: Tapping the right crowd. *Journal of Business Venturing*, 29(5), 585–609. DOI: 10.1016/j.jbusvent.2013.07.003. 31

Bernstein, D. (2013). *Essentials of psychology*. Cengage Learning. 61

Bhattacherjee, A. (2012). Social Science Research: Principles, Methods, and Practices. Book 3.`ht tp://scholarcommons.usf.edu/oa_textbooks/3` 38, 39, 40

Blair, A. (2010). *Too Much to know: Managing scholarly information before the modern age*. Yale University Press. DOI: 10.5860/choice.48-7064. 52

Bonetta, L. (2007). Scientists enter the blogosphere. *Cell*, 129(3), 443–5. DOI: 10.1016/j.cell.2007.04.032. 43

Bonney, R., Cooper, C. B., Dickinson, J., Kelling, S., Phillips, T., Rosenberg, K. V., and Shirk, J. (2009, dec). Citizen Science: A developing tool for expanding science knowledge and scientific literacy. *BioScience*, 59(11), 977–984. DOI: 10.1525/bio.2009.59.11.9. 31

Borgman, C. L. (2007). *Scholarship in the Digital Age: Information, Infrastructure, and the Internet*, (Vol. 6). The MIT Press. DOI: 10.5860/choice.45-4424. 2, 3, 4, 5, 6, 7, 8, 11, 19, 42, 60, 72

Borgman, C. L. (2015). *Big Data, Little Data, No Data: Scholarship in the Networked World*. Cambridge, MA: The MIT Press. DOI: 10.5860/choice.190901. 1, 51, 52

Bouguessa, M., Dumoulin, B., and Wang, S. (2008). Identifying Authoritative Actors in Question-Answering Forums—The Case of Yahoo ! Answers. *Proceedings of the 14th ACM SIGKDD International Conference on Knowledge Discovery and Data Mining*, 866–874. DOI: 10.1145/1401890.1401994. 48

Boyd, D. M. and Ellison, N. B. (2008). Social network sites: definition, history, and scholarship. *Journal of Computer-Mediated Communication*, 13(1), 210–230. DOI: 10.1111/j.1083-6101.2007.00393.x. 15

Boyer, E. L. (1990). *Scholarship reconsidered: Priorities of the professoriate*. New York: Carnegie Foundation for the Advancement of Teaching. 1, 2

Bozzon, A., Brambilla, M., Ceri, S., Silvestri, M., and Vesci, G. (2013). Choosing the Right Crowd: Expert Finding in Social Networks Categories and Subject Descriptors. *Proceedings of the 16th International Conference on Extending Database Technology*, 637–348. DOI: 10.1145/2452376.2452451. 48

Brabham, D. C. (2008). Crowdsourcing as a model for problem solving an introduction and cases. *Convergence: The International Journal of Research into New Media Technologies*, 14(1), 75–90. DOI: 10.1177/1354856507084420. 29

Braghin, S., Yong, J. T. T., Ventresque, A., and Datta, A. (2012). Swat: social web application for team recommendation. In *Parallel and Distributed Systems (icpads)*, *IEEE 18th International Conference on*, (pp. 845–850). DOI: 10.1109/icpads.2012.138. 49

Bronstein, L. R. (2003). A model for interdisciplinary collaboration. *Social Work*, 48(3), 297–306. DOI: 10.1093/sw/48.3.297. 5

Buecheler, T., Sieg, J. H., Füchslin, R. M., and Pfeifer, R. (2010). Crowdsourcing, Open Innovation and Collective Intelligence in the Scientific Method-A Research Agenda and Operational Framework. In *Alife*, (pp. 679–686). 30

Buettner, R. (2015). A Systematic Literature Review of Crowdsourcing Research from a Human Resource Management Perspective. In *System Sciences (hicss)*, *48th Hawaii International Conference on*, (pp. 4609–4618). DOI: 10.1109/hicss.2015.549. 44

Butler, B., Sproull, L., Kiesler, S., and Kraut, R. (2003). Community Effort in Online Groups: Who Does the Work and Why? *Leadership at a Distance*, 1–32. 56

Cameron, D., Aleman-Meza, B., and Arpinar, I. (2007). Collecting expertise of researchers for finding relevant experts in a peer-review setting. Retrieved from `http://corescholar.libr aries.wright.edu/knoesis/215/`. 52

Campos, F. and Valencia, A. (2015). Managing Academic Profiles on Scientific Social Networks. In A. Rocha, A. M. Correia, S. Costanzo, and L. P. Reis (Eds.), *New Contributions in Information Systems and Technologies*, (Vol. 353, pp. 265–273). University of Santiago de Compostela, Spain: Springer. DOI: 10.1007/978-3-319-16486-1_27. 19

Casciaro, T. and Lobo, M. S. (2005). Competent jerks, lovable fools, and the formation of social networks. *Harvard Business Review*, 83(6), 92–99. 52

Casciaro, T. and Lobo, M. S. (2008). When competence is irrelevant: The role of interpersonal affect in task-related ties. *Administrative Science Quarterly*, 53(4), 655–684. DOI: 10.2189/asqu.53.4.655. 52

Chen, B. and Bryer, T. (2012). Investigating Instructional Strategies for Using Social Media in Formal and Informal Learning. *International Review of Research in Open and Distance Learning*, 13(1), 87–104. 56

Cheng, R. and Vassileva, J. (2005). Adaptive reward mechanism for sustainable online learning community. In *Aied*, (pp. 152–159). 63

Clark, H. H. and Brennan, S. E. (1991). Grounding in communication. *Perspectives on Socially Shared Cognition*, 13(1991), 127–149. DOI: 10.1037/10096-006. 7, 47

Clark, H. H. and Wilkes-Gibbs, D. (1986). Referring as a collaborative process. *Cognition*, 22(1), 1–39. DOI: 10.1016/0010-0277(86)90010-7. 47

Collins, E. and Hide, B. (2010). Use and relevance of Web 2.0 resources for researchers. *Methods*, 271–289. 43

Creswell, J. (2009). *Research Design: Qualitative, Quantitative, and Mixed Methods Approaches.* SAGE Publications, Incorporated. 38, 39, 40

Cronin, B., Shaw, D., and La Barre, K. (2003). A cast of thousands: Coauthorship and subauthorship collaboration in the 20th century as manifested in the scholarly journal literature of psychology and philosophy. *Journal of the American Society for information Science and Technology*, 54(9), 855–871. DOI: 10.1002/asi.10278. 5

Cummings, J. N. and Kiesler, S. (2005). Collaborative Research Across Disciplinary and Organizational Boundaries. *Social Studies Of Science*, 703–722. DOI: 10.1177/0306312705055535. 6

David, P. A. and Spence, M. (2003). Towards institutional infrastructures for e-Science: the scope of the challenge. *Information Systems*, (2), 1–98. DOI: 10.2139/ssrn.1325240. 6

Deci, E. L. and Ryan, R. M. (2011). Self-determination theory. *Handbook of Theories of Social Psychology*, 1, 416–433. DOI: 10.4135/9781446249215.n21. 55

DiMicco, J. M. and Millen, D. R. (2007). Identity management: multiple presentations of self in facebook. In *Proceedings of the 2007 International ACM Conference on Supporting Group Work*, (pp. 383–386). DOI: 10.1145/1316624.1316682. 53

Edwards, P. N., Jackson, S. J., Chalmers, M. K., Bowker, G. C., Borgman, C. L., Ribes, D., Burton, M., and Calvert, S. (2013). Knowledge Infrastructures: Intellectual Frameworks and Research Challenges. Ann Arbor: Deep Blue. http://hdl.handle.net/2027.42/97552 69

Edwards, R. (2015). Knowledge infrastructures and the inscrutability of openness in education. *Learning, Media and Technology*, (ahead-of-print), 1–14. DOI: 10.1080/17439884.2015.1006131. 51

Elsayed, A. M. (2015). The Use of Academic Social Networks Among Arab Researchers: A Survey. *Social Science Computer Review*. DOI: 10.1177/0894439315589146. 59, 61

Elsevier. (n.d.). Retrieved from `https://www.elsevier.com/`. 21

Elsevier's policies-article sharing. (n.d.). Retrieved May 31, 2015 from `https://www.elsevier.com/about/company-information/policies/sharing`. 21

Eysenbach, G. (2011). Can tweets predict citations? Metrics of social impact based on Twitter and correlation with traditional metrics of scientific impact. *Journal of Medical Internet Research*, 13(4), e123. DOI: 10.2196/jmir.2012. 18

Fraenkel, J. R., Wallen, N. E., and Hyun, H. H. (1993). *How to Design and Evaluate Research in Education*, (Vol. 7). McGraw-Hill, New York. 38

Friedlander, A. (2009). Asking questions and building a research agenda for digital scholarship. *Working together or apart: Promoting the next generation of digital scholarship*, 1–15. 3

Gagné, M. (2009). A model of knowledge-sharing motivation. *Human Resource Management*, 48(4), 571–589. DOI: 10.1002/hrm.20298. 56

Garvey, W. D. and Griffith, B. C. (1972). Communication and information processing within scientific disciplines: Empirical findings for psychology. *Information Storage and Retrieval*, 8(3), 123–136. DOI: 10.1016/0020-0271(72)90041-1. 6

Goodchild, M. F. and Glennon, J. A. (2010). Crowdsourcing geographic information for disaster response: a research frontier. *International Journal of Digital Earth*, 3(3), 231–241. DOI: 10.1080/17538941003759255. 44

Goodwin, S., Jeng, W., and He, D. (2014). Changing Communication on ResearchGate through Interface Updates. In *Proceedings of the American Society for Information Science and Technology*, (pp. 31–34). DOI: 10.1002/meet.2014.14505101129. 27

Gray, K., Sanchez, F., Bright, G., and Cheng, A. (2013). E-Collaboration in Biomedical Research: Human Factors and Social Media. In *Advancing Medical Practice Through Technology: Applications for Healthcare Delivery, Management, and Quality*, (pp. 102–118). DOI: 10.4018/978-1-4666-4619-3.ch006. 44

Greenhow, C., Robelia, B., and Hughes, J. E. (2009). Learning, teaching, and scholarship in a digital age web 2.0 and classroom research: what path should we take now? *Educational researcher*, 38(4), 246–259. DOI: 10.3102/0013189x09336671. 4

Griffin, S. (2013). *New Roles for Libraries in Supporting Data-Intensive Research and Advancing Scholarly Communication*. Edinburgh, UK: Edinburgh University Press. DOI: 10.3366/ijhac.2013.0060. 3, 4

Gruzd, A., Staves, K., and Wilk, A. (2012). Connected scholars: Examining the role of social media in research practices of faculty using the UTAUT model. *Computers in Human Behavior*, 28(6), 2340–2350. DOI: 10.1016/j.chb.2012.07.004. 41, 42

Gruzd, A., Wellman, B., and Takhteyev, Y. (2011). Imagining Twitter as an Imagined Community. *American Behavioral Scientist*, 55(10), 1294–1318. DOI: 10.1177/0002764211409378. 43, 64

Gu, F. and Widén-Wulff, G. (2011). Scholarly communication and possible changes in the context of social media: A Finnish case study. *The Electronic Library*, 29(6), 762–776. DOI: 10.1108/02640471111187999. 43

Guimerà, R., Uzzi, B., Spiro, J., and Amaral, L. a. N. (2005). Team assembly mechanisms determine collaboration network structure and team performance. *Science*, (New York, N.Y.), 308(5722), 697–702. DOI: 10.1126/science.1106340. 59

Hagstrom, W. O. (1965). *The Scientific Community*. New York: Basic books. 45

Harper, M. (2007). *Encouraging Contributions to Online Communities with Personalization and Incentives*, 1 Promoting Contributions with Incentives, (Vol. 4511). DOI: 10.1007/978-3-540-73078-1_65. 63

Harper, M. F., Weinberg, J., Logie, J., and Konstan, J. A. (2010). Question types in social Q&A sites. *First Monday*, 15(7), 1–19. DOI: 10.5210/fm.v15i7.2913. 27

Haustein, S. and Larivière, V. (2015). The use of bibliometrics for assessing research: possibilities, limitations and adverse effects. In *Incentives and Performance*, (pp. 121–139). Springer. DOI: 10.1007/978-3-319-09785-5_8. 16

Haustein, S., Peters, I., Bar-Ilan, J., Priem, J., Shema, H., and Terliesner, J. (2014). Coverage and adoption of altmetrics sources in the bibliometric community. *Scientometrics*, 101(2), 1145–1163. DOI: 10.1007/s11192-013-1221-3. 19

Hayes, N. (2013). *Doing Qualitative Analysis in Psychology*. Psychology Press. 38

Herrick, D. R. (2009). Google this!: Using Google apps for collaboration and productivity. In *Proceedings of the 37th Annual ACM Siguccs Fall Conference: Communication and Collaboration*, (pp. 55–64). DOI: 10.1145/1629501.1629513. 25

Hicks, A. and Sinkinson, C. (2015). Examining Mendeley: Designing Learning Opportunities for Digital Scholarship. *Libraries and the Academy*, 15(3), 531–549. DOI: 10.1353/pla.2015.0035. 57

Hinds, P. J. and Pfeffer, J. (2003). Why organizations don't "know what they know": Cognitive and motivational factors affecting the transfer of expertise. *Sharing Expertise: Beyond Knowledge Management*, 3–26. 53

Hoffmann, C. P., Lutz, C., and Meckel, M. (2015). A relational altmetric? Network centrality on ResearchGate as an indicator of scientific impact. *Journal of the Association for Information Science and Technology*. DOI: 10.1002/asi.23423. 19

Holmberg, K. and Thelwall, M. (2014). Disciplinary differences in Twitter scholarly communication. *Scientometrics*, 1–16. DOI: 10.1007/s11192-014-1229-3. 59

Howe, J. (2006). The rise of crowdsourcing. *Wired Magazine*, 14(6), 1–4. 29, 30

Hurd, J. M. (2000). The transformation of scientific communication: A model for 2020. *Journal of the American Society for Information Science*, 51(14), 1279–1283. DOI: 10.1002/1097-4571(2000)9999:9999%3C::aid-asi1044%3E3.0.co;2-1. 6

Huysman, M. H. and de Witt, D. (2003). *A Critical Evaluation of Knowledge Management Practices*. 51

Impactstory. (n.d.). Retrieved from https://impactstory.org/ 17

Jeng, W., DesAutels, S., He, D., and Li, L. (2016). Information Exchange on an Academic Social Networking Site: A Multi-discipline Comparison on ResearchGate Q&A. *Journal of the Association for Information Science and Technology*. 70

Jeng, W., He, D., and Jiang, J. (2015). User Participation in an Academic Social Networking Service: A Survey of Open Group Users on Mendeley. *Journal of the Association for Information Science and Technology*, 66(5). DOI: 10.1002/asi.23225. 11, 12, 44, 50, 57, 59, 61

Jenkins, H., Purushotma, R., Weigel, M., Clinton, K., and Robison, A. (2009). *Confronting the challenges of participatory culture: Media education for the 21st century*. The MIT Press. 6

Jiang, J., Ni, C., He, D., and Jeng, W. (2013). Mendeley group as a new source of interdisciplinarity study. *Proceedings of the 13th ACM/IEEE-CS Joint Conference on Digital Libraries–JCDL'13*, 135–138. DOI: 10.1145/2467696.2467738. 45, 57, 59

Kanfer, A. G., Haythornthwaite, C., Bruce, B. C., Bowker, G. C., Burbules, N. C., Porac, J. F., and Wade, J. (2000). Modeling Distributed Knowledge Processes in Next Generation Multidisciplinary Alliances. *Information Systems Frontiers*, 2(3–4), 317–331. DOI: 10.1109/aiworc.2000.843277. 9, 55

Katz, J. and Martin, B. R. (1997). What is research collaboration? *Research Policy*, 26(1), 1–18. DOI: 10.1016/s0048-7333(96)00917-1. 37

Kietzmann, J. H., Hermkens, K., McCarthy, I. P., and Silvestre, B. S. (2011). Social media? Get serious! Understanding the functional building blocks of social media. *Business Horizons*, 54(3), 241–251. DOI: 10.1016/j.bushor.2011.01.005. 24

Kirkup, G. (2010). Academic blogging: academic practice and academic identity. *London Review of Education*, 8(1), 75–84. DOI: 10.1080/14748460903557803. 43

Kogan, M. and Hanney, S. (2000). *Reforming Higher Education*, (Vol. 50). Jessica Kingsley Publishers. 61

Kousha, K. and Thelwall, M. (2014). Disseminating research with Web CV hyperlinks. *Journal of the Association for Information Science and Technology*, 65(8), 1615–1626. DOI: 10.1002/asi.23070. 42

Kraut, R. E., Fussell, S., Brennan, S., and Siegel, J. (2002). Understanding effects of proximity on collaboration: Implications for technologies to support remote collaborative work. *Distributed Work*, 137–162. 47, 52

Kraut, R. E., Galegher, J., and Egido, C. (1987). Relationships and tasks in scientific research collaboration. *Human–Computer Interaction*, 3(1), 31–58. DOI: 10.1207/s15327051hci0301_3. 40

Kraut, R. E., Resnick, P., Kiesler, S., Burke, M., Chen, Y., Kittur, N., Konstan, J., Ren, Y., and Riedl, J. (2012). *Building Successful Online Communities: Evidence-based Social Design*. MIT Press. 62

Lampe, C., Wash, R., Velasquez, A., and Ozkaya, E. (2010). Motivations to participate in online communities. *Proceedings of the SIGCHI Conference on Human Factors in Computing Systems*, 1927–1936. DOI: 10.1145/1753326.1753616. 60

Lampel, J. and Bhalla, A. (2007). The role of status seeking in online communities: Giving the gift of experience. *Journal of Computer-Mediated Communication*, 12, 100–121. DOI: 10.1111/j.1083-6101.2007.00332.x. 61

Lancaster, F. W. (1978). *Toward Paperless Information Systems*. Academic Press, Inc. 6

Latham, G. P. and Pinder, C. C. (2005). Work motivation theory and research at the dawn of the twenty-first century. *Annual Review of Psychology*, 56, 485–516. DOI: 10.1146/annurev.psych.55.090902.142105. 55

Leahey, E. (2007). *Not by Productivity Alone: How Visibility and Specialization Contribute to Academic Earnings*, (Vol. 72). DOI: 10.1177/000312240707200403. 60

Lease, M. and Alonso, O. (2012). Crowdsourcing for search evaluation and social-algorithmic search. In *Proceedings of the 35th International ACM Sigir Conference on Research and Development in Information Retrieval*, (p. 1180). DOI: 10.1145/2348283.2348530. 30

Lee, S., Lee, M., Kim, P., Jung, H., and Sung, W.-K. (2010). OntoFrame s3: semantic web-based academic research information portal service empowered by STAR-WIN. In *The Semantic Web: Research and Applications*, (pp. 401–405). Springer. DOI: 10.1007/978-3-642-13489-0_32. 52

Li, J., Tang, J., Zhang, J., Luo, Q., Liu, Y., and Hong, M. (2007). Eos: expertise oriented search using social networks. In *Proceedings of the 16th International Conference on World Wide Web*, (pp. 1271–1272). DOI: 10.1145/1242572.1242803. 49

Li, X., Thelwall, M., and Giustini, D. (2011). Validating online reference managers for scholarly impact measurement. *Scientometrics*, 91(2), 461–471. DOI: 10.1007/s11192-011-0580-x. 18

Lin, Y.-l., Trattner, C., Brusilovsky, P., and He, D. (2014). The impact of image descriptions on user tagging behavior: A study of the nature and functionality of crowdsourced tags. *Journal of the Association for Information Science and Technology*. DOI: 10.1002/asi.23292. 30

Liu, P., Curson, J., and Dew, P. (2004). Use of RDF for expertise matching within academia. *Knowledge and Information Systems*, 8(1), 103–130. DOI: 10.1007/s10115-004-0152-y. 51

Lu, D., Lu, Y., Jeng, W., Farzan, R., and Lin, Y.-R. (2015). Understanding Health Information Intent via Crowdsourcing: Challenges and Opportunities. *iConference 2015 Proceedings*. 30

Luzón, M. J. (2009). Scholarly hyperwriting: The function of links in academic weblogs. *Journal of the American Society for Information Science and Technology*, 60, 75–89. DOI: 10.1002/asi.20937. 42

Malins, J. and Gray, C. (2013). *Visualizing Research: A Guide to the Research Process in Art and Design*. Ashgate Publishing, Ltd. 38

Maron, N., Kirby Smith, K., and Loy, M. (2009). Sustaining Digital Resources: An On-the-Ground View of Projects Today. *Science*, (July), 136. 43

Marshall, C. C. (2008). From writing and analysis to the repository: taking the scholars' perspective on scholarly archiving. In *Proceedings of the 8th ACM/IEEE-cs Joint Conference on Digital Libraries*, (pp. 251–260). DOI: 10.1145/1378889.1378930. 49

Martin, R. (2011). *We're Gonna Need a Bigger Circle: AKB48 Members Join Google+*. Retrieved from https://www.techinasia.com/akb48-google-plus/. 63

Mathieson, K. (1991). Predicting user intentions: comparing the technology acceptance model with the theory of planned behavior. *Information Systems Research*, 2(3), 173–191. DOI: 10.1287/isre.2.3.173. 56

McDonald, D. W. and Ackerman, M. S. (2000). Expertise recommender: a flexible recommendation system and architecture. *CSCW '00 Proceedings of the 2000 ACM Conference on Computer Supported Cooperative Work*, Philadelphia, 231–240. DOI: 10.1145/358916.358994. 49

Mendeley Global Research report. (2012). Retrieved from http://dfdf.dk/dmdocuments/Mendeley-Global-Research-Report-2012.pdf.

Moilanen, K., Niemi, T., Kuru, M., and Näppilä, T. (2012). A Proposal for a Visual XML Dataspace System. *Journal of Information Science(X)*, 1–22. 18

Moore, D. A., Kurtzberg, T. R., Thompson, L. L., and Morris, M. W. (1999). Long and short routes to success in electronically mediated negotiations: Group affiliations and good vibrations. *Organizational Behavior and Human Decision Processes*, 77(1), 22–43. DOI: 10.1006/obhd.1998.2814. 50

Nández, G. and Borrego, Á. (2013). Use of social networks for academic purposes: a case study. *The Electronic Library*, 31(6), 781–791. DOI: 10.1108/el-03-2012-0031. 41, 42, 43

Neuwirth, C. M., Kaufer, D. S., Chandhok, R., and Morris, J. H. (1990). Issues in the design of computer support for co-authoring and commenting. In *Proceedings of the 1990 ACM Conference on Computer Supported Cooperative Work*, (Vol. 360, pp. 183–195). DOI: 10.1145/99332.99354. 41

Nicholas, D. and Rowlands, I. (2011). Social media use in the research workflow. *Information Services and Use*, 31, 61–83. DOI: 10.1087/20110306. 41, 42, 43, 45

Nielsen, M. (2012). *Reinventing Discovery: The New Era of Networked Science*. Princeton University Press. DOI: 10.1515/9781400839452. 37, 38, 45, 46

NSF. (2013). Retrieved from http://nsf.gov/pubs/policydocs/pappguide/nsf13001/gpg_sigchanges.jsp. 64

Ogata, H., Yano, Y., Furugori, N., and Jin, Q. (2001). Computer Supported Social Networking For Augmenting Cooperation. *Computer Supported Cooperative Work (CSCW)*, 10(2), 189–209. DOI: 10.1023/a:1011216431296. 49

Olson, G. and Olson, J. (2000). Distance Matters. *Human-Computer Interaction*, 15(2), 139–178. DOI: 10.1207/s15327051hci1523_4. 8

Olson, G., Olson, J. and Venolia, G. (2000). What Still Matters About Distance? *Proceedings of HCIC 2009*. x, 7, 8, 9, 28, 37, 49, 71

Olson, G., Zimmerman, A., and Bos, N. (2008). *Scientific Collaboration on the Internet*, (Nos. Book, Whole). MIT Press. DOI: 10.7551/mitpress/9780262151207.001.0001. 6, 9, 37, 47, 52, 71

Olson, J. and Olson, G. (2013). Working together apart: Collaboration over the internet. *Synthesis Lectures on Human-Centered Informatics*, 6(5), 1–151. DOI: 10.2200/s00542ed1v01y201310hci020. 38, 55

Ortega, J. L. (2015). Disciplinary differences in the use of academic social networking sites. *Online Information Review*, 39(4), 520–536. DOI: 10.1108/oir-03-2015-0093.

Panahi, S., Watson, J., and Partridge, H. (2013). Towards tacit knowledge sharing over social web tools. *Journal of Knowledge Management*, 17, 379–397. DOI: 10.1108/jkm-11-2012-0364. 43

Pavlov, M. and Ichise, R. (2007). Finding Experts by Link Prediction in Co-authorship Networks. *FEWS*, 42–55. 49

Pearce, N., Weller, M., Scanlon, E., and Kinsley, S. (2012). Digital scholarship considered: how new technologies could transform academic work. *In education*, 16(1), 33–44. 4

Perez, A. G. and Benjamins, V. R. (1999). Overview of Knowledge Sharing and Reuse Components : Ontologies and Problem-Solving Methods. *IJCAI-99 Workshop on Ontologies and Problem-Solving Method (KRR5)*, 1–15. 51

Perkel, J. M. (2014). Scientific writing: the online cooperative. *Nature*, 514(7520), 127–8. DOI: 10.1038/514127a. 26

Piwowar, H. A. (2013). Value all research products. *Nature*, 493, 159. 64, 68

Piwowar, H. A., Day, R. S., and Fridsma, D. B. (2007). Sharing detailed research data is associated with increased citation rate. *PloS one*, 2(3), e308. DOI: 10.1371/journal.pone.0000308. 60

Plenge, R. M., Greenberg, J. D., Mangravite, L. M., Derry, J. M. J., Stahl, E. A., Coenen, M. J. H., Barton, A., Padyukov, L., Klareskog, L., Gregersen, P. K., Mariette, X., Moreland, L. W., Bridges Jr, S. L., de Vries, N., Huizinga, T. W. J., and Guchelaar, H.-J. (2013). International Rheumatoid Arthritis Consortium (INTERACT), Stephen H. Friend and Gustavo Stolovitzky. Crowdsourcing genetic prediction of clinical utility in the Rheumatoid Arthritis Responder Challenge. *Nature Genetics*, 45(5), 468–469. 30

Porter, C. E. (2004). *A Typology of Virtual Communities: A Multi-Disciplinary Foundation for Future Research*, (Vol. 10). DOI: 10.1111/j.1083-6101.2004.tb00228.x. 60

Priem, J., Piwowar, H. A., and Hemminger, B. M. (2012, mar). Altmetrics in the wild: Using social media to explore scholarly impact. Retrieved from http://arxiv.org/abs/1203.4745. 17, 19

Qin, J., Lancaster, F. W., and Allen, B. (1997). Types and levels of collaboration in interdisciplinary research in the sciences. *Journal of the American Society for Information Science*, 48(10), 893–916. DOI: 10.1002/(sici)1097-4571(199710)48:10%3C893::aid-asi5%3E3.0.co;2-x. 5

Rashid, A. M., Ling, K., Tassone, R. D., Resnick, P., Kraut, R., and Riedl, J. (2006). Motivating participation by displaying the value of contribution. In *Proceedings of the Sigchi Conference on Human Factors in Computing Systems*, (pp. 955–958). DOI: 10.1145/1124772.1124915. 63

Reeve, J. (2014). *Understanding Motivation and Emotion*. John Wiley & Sons. 55, 56

ResearchGate. (n.d.). Retrieved from `https://www.researchgate.net/`. DOI: 10.4016/9522.01. 19, 63

Ross, C., Terras, C., Warwick, M., and Welsh, A. (2011). Enabled Backchannel: Conference Twitter use by Digital Humanists. *Journal of Documentation*, 67, 214–237. DOI: 10.1108/00220411111109449. 42

Rowlands, I., Nicholas, D., and Russell, B. (2011). Social media use in the research workflow. *Information Services & Use*, 31, 61–83. 12

Rowlands, I., Nicholas, D., Russell, B., Canty, N., and Watkinson, A. (2011). Social media use in the research workflow. *Learned Publishing*, 24(3), 183–195. DOI: 10.1087/20110306. 57

Sage's policy of copyright and permissions. (n.d.). Retrieved May 31, 2015 from `https://us.sag epub.com/en-us/nam/copyright-and-permissions`. 21

Schenk, E. and Guittard, C. (2011). Towards a characterization of crowdsourcing practices. DOI: 10.3917/jie.007.0093. 30

Schleyer, T., Butler, B. S., Song, M., and Spallek, H. (2012). Conceptualizing and advancing research networking systems. *ACM Transactions on Computer-Human Interaction*, 19(1), 1–26. DOI: 10.1145/2147783.2147785. 48, 49, 50, 51, 52, 53

Schleyer, T., Spallek, H., Butler, B. S., Subramanian, S., Weiss, D., Poythress, M. L., Rattanathikun, P., and Mueller, G. (2008). Facebook for Scientists: Requirements and Services for Optimizing How Scientific Collaborations Are Established. *Journal of Medical Internet Research*, 10(3), 1–16. DOI: 10.2196/jmir.1047. 11, 48, 49, 52

Shema, H., Bar-Ilan, J., and Thelwall, M. (2012, jan). Research blogs and the discussion of scholarly information. *PloS one*, 7(5), e35869. DOI: 10.1371/journal.pone.0035869. 18, 41

Smith Rumsey, A. (2011). Scholarly communication institute 9: New-model scholarly communication: Road map for change (Tech. Rep.). Charlottesville, VA: University of Virginia Library. Retrieved from `http://www.uvasci.org/wpcontent/uploads/2011/04/SCI9report.pd f`. 3

Springer's self-archiving policy. (n.d.). Retrieved May 31, 2015 from `http://www.springer.c om/gp/open-access/authors-rights/self-archiving-policy/2124`. 21

Suleman, H. and Fox, E. A. (2001). A framework for building open digital libraries. *D-Lib Magazine*, 7(12), 1–9. DOI: 10.1045/december2001-suleman. 70

Sullivan, L. E. (2009). *The sage glossary of the social and behavioral sciences.* Sage. DOI: 10.4135/9781412972024. 55

Tausch, A. (2014). *Researchgate, RG-Scores, or a true Research Gate to Global Research? On the limits of the RG factor and some scientometric evidence on how the current RG score system discriminates against economic and social sciences and against the developing countries.* Retrieved from `https://www.researchgate.net/publication/275647731`. 19

Terveen, L. and McDonald, D. W. (2005). Social matching: A framework and research agenda. *ACM Transactions on ComputerHuman Interaction TOCHI*, 12, 401–434. Retrieved from `http://portal.acm.org/citation.cfm?id=1096737.1096740`. DOI: 10.1145/1096737.1096740. 52

Thelwall, M., Haustein, S., Larivière, V., and Sugimoto, C. R. (2013). Do Altmetrics Work? Twitter and Ten Other Social Web Services. *PLoS One*, 8(5), e64841. Retrieved from `http://dx.plos.org/10.1371/journal.pone.0064841`. DOI: 10.1371/journal.pone.0064841. 11, 18, 19, 60

Thelwall, M. and Kousha, K. (2014). Academia.edu: Social Network or Academic Network? *Journal of the Association for Information Science and Technology*, 65(4), 721–731. DOI: 10.1002/asi.23038. 57

Thelwall, M. and Kousha, K. (2015). ResearchGate : Disseminating, Communicating and Measuring Scholarship? *Journal of the Association for Information Science and Technology*, 66(5), 876–889. DOI: 10.1002/asi.23236. 19, 59

Thij, E. (2007). Online Communities : Exploring Classification Approaches Using Participants' Perspectives. *Communities*, 18–26. 56

Thompson, J. D. (2010). *Organizations in Action: Social Science Bases of Administrative Theory*, (Vol. 1). Transaction Publishers. 37

Tiryakioglu, F. (2011). Use of Social Networks as an Education Tool. *Contemporary Educational Technology*, 2(2), 135–150. Retrieved from `http://www.cedtech.net/articles/223.pdf`. 56

UNESCO. (1999). *The World Communication and Information Report (Tech. Rep.)*. Retrieved from `http://www.unesco.org/webworld/wcir/en/`. 2

Unsworth, J. (2000). Scholarly primitives: What methods do humanities researchers have in common, and how might our tools reflect this. In *Humanities Computing, Formal Methods, Experimental Practice Symposium*, (pp. 5–100). 2

Van House, N. A. (2004). Science and technology studies and information studies. *Annual Review of Information Science and Technology*, 38(1), 1–86. DOI: 10.1002/aris.1440380102. 51

Van Rijnsoever, F. J. and Hessels, L. K. (2011). Factors associated with disciplinary and interdisciplinary research collaboration. *Research Policy*, 40(3), 463–472. DOI: 10.1016/j.respol.2010.11.001. 5

Vassileva, J. (2005). Adaptive incentive mechanism for sustainable online community. In *Proceedings of Workshop "Sustaining Community: The Role and Design of Incentive Mechanisms in Online Systems" at ACM Group 2005 Conference*. 61, 62

Vassileva, J. (2012). Motivating participation in social computing applications: a user modeling perspective. *User Modeling and User-Adapted Interaction*, 22(1–2), 177–201. DOI: 10.1007/s11257-011-9109-5. 63

Veletsianos, G. and Kimmons, R. (2012). Networked participatory scholarship: emergent technocultural pressures toward open and digital scholarship in online networks. *Computers & Education*, 58(2), 766–774. DOI: 10.1016/j.compedu.2011.10.001. 1, 6, 11, 45, 60

Wang, G. A., Jiao, J., Abrahams, A. S., Fan, W., and Zhang, Z. (2013). ExpertRank: A topic-aware expert finding algorithm for online knowledge communities. *Decision Support Systems*, 54(3), 1442–1451. DOI: 10.1016/j.dss.2012.12.020. 48

Weber, G. M., Barnett, W., Conlon, M., Eichmann, D., Kibbe, W., Falk-Krzesinski, H., Halaas, M., Johnson, L., Meeks, E., Mitchell, D. and Schleyer, T. (2011). Direct2Experts: a pilot national network to demonstrate interoperability among research-networking platforms. *Journal of the American Medical Informatics Association*. Retrieved from http://www.ncbi.nlm.nih.gov/pubmed/22037890. DOI: 10.1136/amiajnl-2011-000200. 11

Weller, M. (2011). *The Digital Scholar: How Technology is Transforming Academic Practice*. Bloomsbury Academic. DOI: 10.5040/9781849666275. 29, 64

Wiggins, A. Crowston, K. (2011). From conservation to crowdsourcing: A typology of citizen science. In *System Sciences (Hicss), 44th Hawaii International Conference on*, (pp. 1–10). DOI: 10.1109/hicss.2011.207. 31

Wiley's self-archiving policy. (n.d.). Retrieved May 31, 2015 from http://olabout.wiley.com/WileyCDA/Section/id-820227.html. 21

Yang, S. J. H. and Chen, I. Y. L. (2008). A social network-based system for supporting interactive collaboration in knowledge sharing over peer-to-peer network. *International Journal of Human-Computer Studies*, 66(1), 36–50. DOI: 10.1016/j.ijhcs.2007.08.005. 49

Yuan, P., Bare, M. G., Johnson, M. O., and Saberi, P. (2014). Using online social media for recruitment of human immunodeficiency virus-positive participants: A cross-sectional survey. *Journal of Medical Internet Research*, 16(May), 1–11. DOI: 10.2196/jmir.3229. 44

Zahedi, Z., Costas, R., and Wouters, P. (2014). How well developed are altmetrics? A cross-disciplinary analysis of the presence of 'alternative metrics' in scientific publications. *Scientometrics*, (Haustein 2010), 1–16. DOI: 10.1007/s11192-014-1264-0. 60

Zheng, J. (2002). Trust without Touch: Jumpstarting long-distance trust with initial social activities. *Proceedings of CHI2002*, 141–146. DOI: 10.1145/503376.503402. 50

Authors' Biographies

DAQING HE

Daqing He (dah44@pitt.edu) is an associate professor at the School of Information Sciences (iSchool), and associate professor at the Intelligent Systems Program, both of which are at the University of Pittsburgh. He earned his Ph.D. degree in artificial intelligence from the University of Edinburgh, Scotland. Prior joining the University of Pittsburgh in 2004, he served on the research faculties of the Robert Gordon University, Scotland and the University of Maryland at College Park, College Park, MD. His main research interests cover information retrieval (monolingual and multilingual), information access on the social web, adaptive web systems and user modeling, interactive retrieval interface design, web log mining and analysis, and research data management. Dr. He has been the Principal Investigator (PI) and Co-PI for more than ten research projects, funded by the National Science Foundation (NSF), United States Defense Advanced Research Projects Agency (DARPA), University of Pittsburgh, and other agencies. He has published more than 120 articles in internationally recognized journals and conferences in these areas, which include *Journal of Association for Information Science and Technology, Information Processing and Management, ACM Transaction on Information Systems, Journal of Information Science*, ACM SIGIR, CIKM, WWW, CSCW, and so on. Dr. He has served as a member on the program committees for more than 30 major international conferences in the area of information retrieval and web technologies, and has been called upon to be a reviewer for many top-ranked international journals in the same areas. He services on the editorial board of SCI/SSCI indexed journals *Internet Research* and *Aslib Journal of Information Management*.

WEI JENG

Wei Jeng (wej9@pitt.edu) is a Ph.D. student in the School of Information Sciences (iSchool) at the University of Pittsburgh. Her research explores how people share information, data, and resources in the digital age. Given the increasing need in academic communities to manage a huge amount of data, her long-term research goal is to provide insights on improving research infrastructure for scholars in all disciplines, particularly social sciences, humanities, and related scholarly communities.

Printed in the United States
by Baker & Taylor Publisher Services